SITTING WITH SUFIS

SITTING WITH
SUFIS

A Christian Experience
of Learning Sufism

MARY BLYE HOWE

PARACLETE PRESS
BREWSTER, MASSACHUSETTS

Published in association with the literary agency of Alive Communications, Inc., 7680 Goddard Street, Suite 200, Colorado Springs, CO 80920.

Library of Congress Cataloging–in–Publication Data

Howe, Mary Blye.
  Sitting with Sufis : a Christian experience of learning Sufism / Mary Blythe Howe.
      p. cm. — (Many mansions)
  Includes bibliographical references (p. 123).
  ISBN 1–55725–415–X
    1. Howe, Mary Blye. 2. Spiritual biography. 3. Sufism. 4. Christianity and other religions—Sufism. I. Title. II. Series
      BL73.H69 A3 2005
      297.4'092—dc22

2005 First Printing

10   9   8   7   6   5   4   3   2   1

Published by Paraclete Press
Brewster, Massachusetts
www.paracletepress.com

Printed in the United States of America

For

Sherif Catalkaya

AND

Shahabuddin David Less

CONTENTS

THIS BOOK IS INTENDED TO BE A SPIRITUAL MEMOIR, not a treatise on Sufism. My spiritual practices are my own and don't necessarily reflect Sufism as a whole, or even the practices of the order with which I am affiliated. Though I've carefully checked my facts and made corrections based on feedback from Sufi friends, my experiences and reflections are personal.

All quotations from existing works, including all biblical quotations, are referenced in a set of endnotes at the conclusion of the text. The complete information on these references is included in the bibliography. Also many of the italicized terms in the text are further explained in the glossary following the endnotes.

CHAPTER ONE

Longing for God

*M*y Mom delights in telling the story of the morning she stood on the porch of our white-shingled house in a coal-mining town in southern Illinois watching me ride my tricycle. As a three-year-old, I was vigorously pedaling from one end of our front sidewalk to the other. When I'd come to the street at one end, I'd pause, gaze into the sky, and wave. Then reversing my direction, my tiny legs turning the pedals as rapidly as possible, I'd reach the street at the other end of the sidewalk. Once again I'd pause, look upward, and wave.

Mom watched me for a long time. Back and forth I went, pedaling with all my might, then stopping and waving toward the sky.

Finally, Mom called to me. "Mary Blye. What are you doing, honey?"

"Waving to God," I called back.

This story symbolizes my spiritual and religious journey. For as long as I can remember, a deep awareness of and a longing for God has existed within my heart. The home in which I grew up, and the church of my childhood, emphasized the eternal, undying love of God, and so before I could even read or write, it felt natural for me to "wave" to God. My childhood mentors—my family and church—depicted God as my dearest Friend.

When my mother had discovered that she was pregnant with me, nearly twenty years after she'd birthed her first child and ten years after her last, she believed it was something of a miracle. So each morning from then on, my mom drove to the First Baptist Church, parked her car, walked into the empty sanctuary, knelt at the altar, and dedicated me to God. Just two weeks after my birth, my parents began taking me to church, and so began the many years of my faithful attendance, three times a week, every week—throughout my childhood and long into my adult years.

My childhood memories of church are filled with warmth and love. I still remember my preschool teacher, Mrs. Gilchrist, who tenderly cuddled me in her arms and sang softly about Jesus. My other Sunday school teachers also inspired me to love God. I sang in the children's choir, proudly took home my artwork, checked off the box on my Sunday school envelope that told my teachers I'd read my Bible each day, set aside a tithe of my money, and prayed.

Yet as I grew older I realized that somewhere along the way I had stopped waving to God. As a young adult I entered a period of my life when I became obsessed with the outward forms of goodness and nearly lost the deeper spiritual truths, which I was to discover were embedded within all of the great religions of the world. Because I had gone through a period of teenage rebellion, I gravitated toward a church that would act as a harsh, correcting parent, so to speak, giving me clear rules and guidelines to follow, along with a black-and-white definition of morality. Thus the letter of the law began to consume my life, and the pronouncements of God's judgment soon obliterated the message of grace and love with which I'd grown up.

This period carried over into my mid-thirties. Then a new church brought a fresh vision of God into the tiny corner in which I'd been hovering. In addition, after attending an interfaith service,

I became captivated by Judaism. Jewish prayer services gave me a powerful sense of the presence of God. The Jewish approach to study, in which dozens of questions are raised and explored, opened me to new ways of thinking about and experiencing God. The rituals in Judaism seemed filled with mystery and spiritual meaning. I began to hear, once again, God's still, small voice, whispering into my consciousness the vast and breathtaking realm of the divine.

Slowly I began wiping away the cobwebs and venturing out, tentatively at first, then more enthusiastically. I discovered that God really didn't fit neatly into the box I had put God in for so long. As I opened myself to ideas about God that were different from my own, I realized I didn't hold all the answers, and that my experience of God wasn't the only valid one.

A few days ago I was describing this period of my life to a reporter who had called to interview me for a story for a San Francisco periodical. As I detailed these years for him, relating how my closed, unquestioning mind had shut me off to genuine spiritual growth, he asked the question that had been puzzling him: "So what prompted you to change? In all of this, there must have remained some kind of openness. What happened?"

It was a good question, and the answer lies both in my story of waving at God and in what the Sufis call *zikr*, or Divine Remembrance. Sufism is a mystical practice that emphasizes certain unique rituals for guiding spiritual seekers into a direct encounter with God, and *zikr* is one of its most important rituals. Thus through a series of circumstances which I'll describe later in this book, God called me back to the time when I simply gazed into the heavens with wonder, awe, and love. In the midst of the isolated religious world I'd created within and without, I suddenly remembered the God of my early years.

Now, ten years later, I feel a tremendous sense of freedom and joy. My spiritual life is a rich blend, even as I feel drawn to and at home with some religious traditions over others. Christianity is my family, and the church is the place where I celebrate Jesus and honor the special place he holds in my life.

Along with church services, I also regularly attend synagogue services, a practice I began after a Jewish congregation invited my church to participate in an interfaith service which piqued my interest in Judaism. I've grown to love Judaism and I honor the unique place it holds in my life.

Yet while Christianity and Judaism were strengthening my relationship with God, I began to yearn for a spiritual path that would lead me deeper into the mysteries of faith and would allow me to taste the esoteric worlds of which the great mystics wrote. I longed to plunge beneath the surface of religion, into the mysteries that lie at its heart. I wanted a spiritual path with greater depth, rituals, and disciplines that would lead me through the mystical worlds, or spiritual levels, experienced by the mystics. I grew to cherish the ecumenism, unity, and love that the mystics emphasize.

Because I'd spent most of my life thinking in terms of black and white, with little mystery, and few questions, I felt deeply drawn to the mystical life of Sufism, with its particular rituals, passion, lack of dogma, and its poets and teachers, that intensely attracted me.

The branch with which I chose to affiliate has a universal emphasis. Before I received initiation, for instance, I sat down with the *shaykh* who is now my Sufi teacher and asked him if being a dervish, as Sufis are more commonly called, would conflict with my connection to Christianity and Judaism.

"Sufism can be practiced within any religion," Sherif Baba told me. "It is the heart of religion."

Since that day, I've heard Baba refer several times to a famous poem by Rumi, Sufism's most well-known poet.

Mevlana [Rumi] was raised as a Muslim but when he said, "Come, come!" he wasn't calling people to Islam. He was calling out to humanity. He brought a love and unity among people that is spreading light everywhere, in the East and in the West.

Many Sufis whom I know aren't affiliated with any religion, some are, and that's one of the many lovely things about Sufism—at least in the orders (branches or lineages) with which I'm affiliated. Sufism honors the individual's special relationship to a particular religion, prophet, or religious leader.

As Hazrat Inayat Khan, the Indian master who brought Sufism to the West, wrote, "[The Sufi Movement has] members . . . which belong to all the different religions, for all are welcome: Christians, Buddhists, Parsis, Muslims. No one's faith or belief is questioned; each can follow his own church, religion, creed."

In the spirit of these words, Sufism is teaching me to glean the gems and treasures from Christianity—to reach into its essence and live the teaching of Jesus and of the Hebrew prophets. "Teacher, which commandment in the law is the greatest?" someone once asked Jesus. He replied, reiterating the beloved *shema* of the Jews, "You shall love the Lord your God with all your heart, and with all your soul, and with all your mind." "This," Jesus said, "is the greatest and first commandment." Then, continuing to quote from the Hebrew Scripture, he added, "And a second is like it: 'You shall love your neighbor as yourself.' On these two commandments hang all the law and the prophets."

The strongest attraction of Sufism for me has been, though, its emphasis on the romance of Divine Love. Rumi, who is currently America's best-selling poet, writes this:

O lovers! O lovers!
I can turn dust into diamonds!
O minstrels! O minstrels!
I can fill your tambourines with gold!

O thirsty souls! O thirsty souls!
I can give you water to drink
I can turn this dustbin into the flowing waters of paradise!

As a child, I remember most vividly my fascination with the Hebrew prophets. They described a God who would stop at nothing to win the heart of the beloved. Nothing could deter this God, nothing hamper such passionate, Divine love. The prophets often spoke of the relationship of God with humankind as that of Lover and Beloved. Such romance drew me, even at a young age.

When I encountered Sufism, I knew I'd found the path that would lead me, step by step, with the practice of Sufi rituals, disciplines, and meditations, into this Divine Romance. Rumi beckoned me to "Come, come!" Come and drink the wine of the Beloved; become inebriated with God.

"I follow the religion of Love," wrote Rumi, "and go whichever way his camel leads me." Because love is at the heart of all the great religions, I knew this was the path that could lead me to the essence of faith, and allow me to discover the bonds that unite us as human beings.

Soon I was praying daily the words of Hazrat Inayat Khan, "Raise us above the distinctions and differences which divide us." The distinctions of personalities and religions don't disappear in their outward form, but mysticism takes us to the center where the differences do, indeed, disappear.

While the practices of Sufism have provided me with a unique spiritual path, these practices have also offered me a deeper mystical entryway, as well as a more vibrant sense of divine love, within the religions I most love. Sufism hasn't replaced religion; it has deepened it. Sufism is helping me learn again to wave at God.

When I was struggling with the decision of whether to receive initiation onto the path of Sufism, a friend told me to stop worrying about it. I could, so to speak, drink and eat at their table, nourishing myself as a guest for as long as I wanted.

This is what I offer to you. Sup at the table of the dervishes. Be a guest, have a few *hors d'oeuvres*, and nibble from the feast that has been prepared. Your life will be changed, your experience of God expanded, and your heart opened. And one day you may find yourself so full that you can no longer leave the table.

CHAPTER TWO

Discovering
the Dervishes

*O*ne of my own first nibbles at the table of the
dervishes came when I danced with God
under a huge canopy at a lovely 720-acre
ranch in the Texas hill country. Though I'd taken part in many
religious and spiritual rituals within Judaism and Christianity, I
knew little about the rituals of the Sufis. I'd soon learn, though,
that the purpose is the same: to become absorbed, along with
other like-minded seekers, in God, and to leave that place of
worship with a more lasting, deeper sense of God's presence in
one's daily life.

Here is my memory of that evening. . . .

It's nearing midnight and we've just finished a ritual called
zikr (also known as *dhikr*)—an important Sufi ritual in which one
remembers God through meditational chant and movement. In
zikr we repeat certain Divine Names of God, representing
attributes of God such as mercy and kindness, so that our hearts
and lives may become more saturated with the characteristics of
God.

Although it's late and we've been immersed in *zikr* since
around 8:00, few of us want the evening to end. My heart feels
baptized in God's presence. After sitting quietly for a while, one of

the teachers, Shahabuddin David Less, motions for us to stand. "Do we want sleep," he asks, "or do we want ecstasy?" "Ecstasy!" everyone calls back. (Shahabuddin had asked the same question another time, right before lunch, asking whether we wanted food or ecstasy, and someone from the crowd asked if we had to choose.)

Ecstasy, in my experience, is a feeling utterly unlike any other. During my teen years I was often high on drugs, and at different periods of my life I've been on emotional highs. But the ecstatic state of the mystic is entirely different. Rabbi David Cooper points out that this state of consciousness shatters and transforms us. Hazrat Inayat Khan writes of ecstasy as a state of purity in which our hearts are conscious only of God. St. Francis fell into ecstasy when "his heart received the meaning and power" of the divine words of God.

During *zikr*, when we receive in our hearts the meaning and power of the Divine Names, or Attributes, of God, a deeper sense of the presence of God envelops us and, to some degree, changes us permanently.

So this evening, more than one hundred people fill the canvas floor, doing a form of the *sema*, the movement which Jelaluddin Rumi, Sufism's most famous poet, originated, and which the dervishes from Konya, Turkey, known as the "whirling dervishes," currently present to audiences all over the world.

I, however, along with a few other people, hold back. I don't know the movement (it's highly symbolic), and I'm not as uninhibited as most people here seem to be. I'm also unaccustomed to spiritual practices outside of Christianity and Judaism, thus making me nervous about engaging in a ritual that I'm unfamiliar with.

As I sit trying to talk myself out of participating, I suddenly find myself drawn into the vortex. With my right hand symbolically raised

towards heaven and the palm of my left hand facing the earth—
representing the intertwining of the two worlds—I begin to whirl.

A beautiful segment of Rumi's poetry put to music by Jeff
Olmsted springs to mind:

> Oh, I absorb the shining!
> And now I am the ocean,
> Millions of simultaneous motions
> moving everywhere, moving in me!

And then another:

> Dance when you're broken open,
> Dance, if you've torn the bandage off.
> Dance in the middle of the fighting.
> Dance in your blood.
> Dance when you're perfectly free.
> Dance!

And that's what I did, losing a sense of time, forgetting my
self-consciousness, and dissolving the barriers that exist between
the sacred and the profane.

My entire adult life had been steeped in fundamentalism, but
during the past several years a new church, Judaism, and the
mystical path of Sufism were gradually setting me free. This dance
was symbolic of the freedom I'd found in discovering new aspects
of God. I had "torn the bandage off."

....

My journey began in a surprising manner. Some years back, I
had returned to school to pursue a degree in philosophy and
anthropology and had, toward the end of my studies, signed up
for a class on Neoplatonism, a form of mysticism. Though several
classes would turn out to have a profound effect on my life, this

particular class piqued more than my interest. It plunged me into mystical studies, and then later, into mystical experiences. The class, taught by Dr. Tim Mahoney, delved into such mystical ideas as *emanation*—the idea that successive levels of creation sprang from the "the One"—as well as into various concepts of ascent, or return to God, which I'll describe in detail in a later chapter. To the Neoplatonists, God couldn't be adequately described in words nor experienced with the intellect.

Although our primary focus of study involved the Christian and pagan Neoplatonists, I learned from my outside readings that some of these mystical beliefs were similar to those of other religions—certain sects of Buddhists, Jews, and Muslims, Hindus in general, and several other religions. Looking for articles and announcements that indicated what mystical groups might be meeting in Dallas, where I live, I began subscribing to local *listservs* and visiting different places of worship.

Then one day I received a brochure in the mail about a Sufi retreat in Austin. I had read some of Rumi's poetry, but I knew almost nothing of Sufism beyond that. I sent a check and registered for the weekend. When the time arrived, I packed my bags and drove to the ranch.

Again my memory takes me back to that day I whirled with the dervishes. . . .

Arriving at the ranch, I turn off the main road and wind along bumpy, dirt roads that lead into the ranch. I rarely have seen land in Texas that evokes the word *beauty*, but this place does. Clear water bounds down a large creek, twisting between a forest of Spanish oaks and junipers. Massive windows cover one side of a lovely home, and a deck sprawls over an inlet where a large expanse of water pools alongside boulders and gently sloping inclines.

Don Hejny, the manager of the ranch, motions for me to drive across the creek. His facial expression radiates a quiet joy. Bracing myself, I plunge my car into the water and bounce across, up a short but steep hill and around a corner, where I almost run over two men dancing in the middle of the road.

Tents sprawl alongside the creek's bank, and people walk back and forth, unloading their cars, rocking in long embraces, and getting settled in tents and various rooms in the home with the large windows. The chatter coming from underneath a massive tarp is already drawing people in, as the musicians and sound men test their voices and equipment. Most people are dressed in everyday clothes, though some women wear saris (a traditional Indian dress), or attire that represents other countries such as Israel or Turkey.

Nervously, I park my car and walk down to the tent, taking my seat towards the back. Sufi masters from two different orders (branches or lineages of Sufism) sit in folding chairs, along with a few other people who will be leading different parts of the weekend retreat. For a few minutes, everyone sits quietly, breathing in the tranquil atmosphere of our surroundings. The teachers gaze at us, smiling, comfortable with both silence and eye contact. I'm drawn to each of them immediately.

Shahabuddin, a Sufi master from Florida, begins the morning with a question. "Who are you? Why are you here?" In Sufism, *muhasaba*—or self-analysis—is an extremely important discipline, and Shahabuddin's question is one that Sufis, like those in other religious traditions, attempt to continually ask themselves.

Shahabuddin wears a *kurta*—a long, Indian-style shirt, and has bundled his long, gray hair into a ponytail. An expression of holy delight fills his face—an expression that I have found only on the faces of authentic spiritual leaders. Soon we begin the Sufi practice called *sohbet*, or spiritual discourse, in which Sufis listen to the teachings and stories of spiritual masters, and also respond to their questions. Sufi masters don't prepare, edit, or rehearse their lessons. Rather, Sufi discourse springs spontaneously from the heart—a heart immersed in hours of daily meditation and reflection.

Sohbet is a time when Sufi masters share the wisdom that comes from a heart habitually and deeply attuned to God. I've now sat through hundreds of *sohbets* and without exception, I've come away from each one knowing I've been brought into a deeper level of spirituality, and into a more intimate and lasting encounter with God.

This particular morning, before the Sufi masters begin *sohbet*, we sing. Pandit Mukesh Desai, a renowned Indian musician, sits on a cushion, and a few tones resonate from his harmonium. Mukesh's voice blends with the instrument's slow, melodic tones, his free hand moving through the air as if he were pulling in the music, then releasing it, pulling, then releasing.

Music works spiritual magic. On Sunday mornings in church, the majesty of the organ automatically ceases our chatter, and before the service has even begun, my soul seems to rise to a higher realm of being. When I attend synagogue, as I often do, I'm struck by the holiness of "musical" prayers—prayers that we melodically chant or sing. In *The Secret of Francis of Assisi*, author Christian Bobin writes that "music [drags] God from His slumbers."

Singing, then, changes our frame of mind, and this morning it was opening me to the spiritual discourse from another Sufi teacher—a Turkish shaykh named Sherif Catalkaya, whom everyone calls *Baba* (a Turkish term of affection, meaning Dad).

"Aşk öyle bir güneştir, ki kalbi yumuşak toprağa çevirir."

"Love is such a sun that it turns the heart into soft earth," Baba says.

"Bu yolu yürümeye çalışıyoruz . . . "

"This is the path we're trying to walk. And we walk it through the presence of the Beloved." Baba wears a mixture of Western and Turkish clothing, along with a colorful Turkish hat known as a *takke*. He fingers his prayer beads as he talks.

When he speaks, an atmosphere of kindness and joy fills the room. His eyes are full of divine joy, his mouth etched in a continuous smile that seems almost mischievous. The first moment I met Baba, I instinctively knew I could do or say anything around him and he'd still love me. He seemed both divinely radiant and utterly comfortable to be with.

Though Baba knows enough English to carry on a basic conversation, he's more comfortable speaking his native Turkish. Because of this, his translator, Jem, is his right arm. A man nearly as tall as a professional basketball player, Jem has wild, waist-length, red hair and a mustache that sweeps nearly from ear to ear. Jem spontaneously matches Baba's cadence, gestures, and facial expressions as he translates, even as his own lovely personality shines through.

Baba is a masterful storyteller, delighting me with both his natural humor and the deep meaning he brings to all of his stories.

"Bir zamanlar size hikaye anlatmıştım ."

"I once told you a story."

"Eğer müsade ederseniz bu hikayeyi bir daha anlatayım."

"If you give me permission, let me tell the story again."

Baba then tells of a dervish in Istanbul who had no money and couldn't find work. "One day he tells his friends, 'I'm going to write Allah a letter and ask him for money.'

"His friends say, 'How can you write Allah a letter? What address are you going to send it to? How will the money get to you? Will it fall out of the sky?'

"The dervish was so pure," Baba explains, "living the beauty of Allah, that he simply told his friends, 'I know Allah's address.' Then he wrote the letter:

'Dear Allah, I can't find any work and my family is hungry, so send me fifty lire.' The dervish puts the letter in an envelope and takes it to the post office."

Baba continues: "After the mail is sorted, one of the mail handlers sees the letter. It's addressed: Dear Allah, City of la mekan şehir (the non-existent city). The mail handler is afraid to open it so he takes it to the postmaster, who reads it and cries. The letter was written with *so* much sincerity," says Baba, "that the compassion of the man reading becomes inflamed.

"So he takes the letter and puts fifty lire in it and puts this man's address on the envelope. On the back he writes, 'Sent by Allah.' And he sends it.

"The man gets the envelope and he's very happy. He shows his friends the money. 'You see,' he says, 'I knew Allah's address.'

"This is how Allah works," says Baba, "through sincerity and compassion. When people live with these, they go into action and *ashk* [divine love] is manifested. If that man had not written the letter with sincerity and the other man had not read it with compassion, there would have been no *ashk*. He would have thought, 'this man is crazy,' and he would have torn up the letter and thrown it away. But sincerity joined with compassion brought *ashk* into being."

Through stories like this, I would learn that this kind of divine love—*ashk*—is the central aspect of Sufism. Indeed, I've come to believe that *ashk* is at the heart of all religion and spirituality.

············

As we move through the weekend, I find myself becoming more and more comfortable. Vegetarian feasts, which have taken hours to prepare, fill the picnic tables on the front lawn. As I chat with different people during our meals, I discover that most live typical lives: working, taking care of families, and searching for spiritual satisfaction.

One afternoon, during a break, I sit with Baba and Jem on the patio and ask them about Sufism. The idea of having a spiritual teacher to guide me along a mystical path, allowing me to experience God in new ways, appeals to me, but I'm filled with questions. As Jem translates, Baba leans forward, nods and smiles broadly, and eagerly answers all my questions.

After our talk, I pass part of the afternoon walking around the ranch. Several people swim in the creek; others nap on couches, walk through the woods, or read. After a music class with Mukesh, we eat again. In the evening, *zikr*—Divine Remembrance—begins.

During *zikr*, which is one of the most important aspects of Sufism, we chant some of the ninety-nine Divine Names of God, representing various attributes of God. Though ninety-nine is the traditional number, in reality, God's Names/Attributes are infinite.

All Sufi orders practice *zikr*, though how they do so varies among the different orders. At least one order practices a "silent" *zikr*, but most chant aloud, accompanied by symbolic movement. Some orders use sacred dance, rich in symbolism. Often, movements begin at a slow, measured pace, then gradually pick up in tempo.

As I participate in this ritual, I find myself entering a holy place within, a place where I sense the presence of God in a powerful way. My self-consciousness dissolves. Until now, I've felt God most powerfully when I'm by myself, probably because that's where I can most easily let myself go. But here, along with others, I melt into a single Source, with all of our differences absorbed by the power of Divine Love.

The next morning I'm still buzzing as we end the weekend with a ceremony called Universal Worship, a ritual which at least one Sufi order practices regularly. After it's over, I sit unable to move, weeping openly. Margaret Hejny comes over to me and gently asks if I'm OK. Before I can answer, she smiles and says, "Never mind. I can see in your eyes that you are."

·········

During my solo drive back to Dallas, I remain filled with the spirit of the weekend. I had been looking for a group that regularly met together to engage in mystical practices, and I'm excited because I've found one.

At home, I begin buying books on Sufism. I buy Sufi poetry, philosophy, compilations of stories, biographies, and books that describe Sufi rituals and practices.

Over the weekend, I discovered that one of the participants, Wahhaba Phillips, lives close to me and leads Sufi activities each week, and I begin attending these.

One evening, I visit a Sufi group unfamiliar to me and discover that I, as a woman, have to sit in the back of the room. I never return to this group.

A Christian friend from Iran, Samira Izadi, who grew up in a Sufi home, recommends that I visit an Iranian Sufi group that she and her husband, Hassan, are familiar with, and I do. One evening each week, this group holds an "American" evening, in which men and women sit together. The teaching is profound and the meditation leaves me with a sense of complete serenity.

Yet while Sufism is my primary mystical path, I continue to cherish both Christianity and Judaism. Among the revered saints in the Christian tradition, St. Teresa, in particular, fascinates me, and I long to visit Avila. St. Francis, also, holds a special place in my heart, and last year, during my husband's and my twenty-fifth wedding anniversary, we spent time in Assisi, pausing for prayer and reflection high on the mountain where St. Francis communed with God through nature, and with the birds, deer, and the other animals that felt safe and comfortable with him.

Increasingly, I feel the spirit of the mystics flowing through me, creating a more finely tuned spirituality and filling me with a new serenity. Sufism instills in me a sense that I'm intimately connected with all of humankind—indeed, with all of creation—and it teaches me the path of divine union with God. That path has instilled in me a powerful longing for a pure and holy heart, saturated continually with the presence of God.

CHAPTER THREE

Unveiling My Heart

*A*utumn is in full eruption as I drive through the Black Mountains, the Smokies, and other parts of the Appalachians on my way to North Carolina where Baba, who has become my Sufi teacher, leads a community of about fifty people in Chapel Hill. I'm thinking of the Sufi's emphasis on the heart and sense my own heart softening and opening in anticipation of the week I'll be spending with my dervish friends.

In Sufism, as in Judaism, Christianity, and other religions, the heart is of the utmost importance because it's seen as the spiritual center of our being, the place where God dwells. Sufism teaches that the heart must be purified, and one of the ways Sufis do this is through *zikr*, a ritual used to imprint God continuously on your heart. Through forgetfulness of God, the heart can become veiled and we can be misled, but the heart itself—the deepest part of our being—is trustworthy. It's the place we find God and thus, the place we should trust that our guidance will come from. I'll be reminded of this in many ways throughout the retreat.

When I arrive in the general vicinity of Chapel Hill, I phone Demir, Jem's brother, and he tells me to meet him at his Turkish rug shop. I'll then follow him to the camp. At the shop, a large group of people who have arrived from Turkey for the community's

annual event, called "Rumi Fest," mill about in the parking lot.
I'm amused that only a few years ago, at a Jewish holiday celebration, I had found myself at a party where everyone spoke Russian.
Now here I am at a Sufi retreat where everyone appears to be
speaking Turkish.

Soon Demir arrives, and we all pile into our cars and follow
him to a lovely, wooded place where the retreat will take place. We
walk a bit, find out where we're staying, and then head to our
hotel rooms for a brief rest.

Though most of Baba's community in Chapel Hill isn't
Turkish, Baba and his guests from Turkey bring their vivacious
culture to the forefront. If our eyes meet during *sohbet*, the
Turkish women smile and place a hand over their hearts, a gesture
that has a variety of meanings, but is often used by Sufis to indicate
affection. During the conference, the women often come up to me,
touch my arm shyly, and wave. Since we speak different languages,
that's the only way we can communicate.

It rains hard for most of the weekend (several of us have to
have our cars dug out from the mud), but Baba gets off to his usual
exuberant start: "This morning I said to Allah, 'Take away the
rain!' But Allah didn't listen to me. Allah listened to the earth!"

Baba then begins to teach us. "If we want to gain the *Nur*
[divine light] of Allah, then we must connect to Allah with love
and sincerity. The Creator is telling us in every breath, 'I am with
you,' and is asking us, 'Who are you with?'

"To be a true friend of Allah," Baba reminds us, "is to live
Allah in your heart."

Jesus and many of the Hebrew prophets placed the greatest
emphasis on the heart. One must believe with the heart, love with
the heart, forgive from the heart, and obey and serve with the
heart. Repentance must be from the heart. We're told by Moses to

"circumcise" our hearts, and by other biblical writers to give thanks with our "whole heart", and to love not only God, but one another "deeply from the heart." For Jesus and for the Hebrew prophets, going through the empty motions of religion without experiencing God with all of your heart wasn't genuine religion.

Because of the mystics' emphasis on the heart, the attitude towards the intellect and study is often misunderstood by those who know little about mysticism. Many mystics have been great scholars. However, none of them believed you could find God through mere study. You had to go *beyond* study. Intellect and study are good. Learning about God is good. But neither intellect nor learning will take you into the direct presence of God which, to the mystic, is the ultimate goal. Rumi, whom I consider to be Sufism's greatest and most passionate poet, possessed a heart that seemed literally oblivious to anything but God. "Drain passion's cup," he wrote, "and be not ashamed; Close off the head's gaze, [and] see instead the hidden eye."

Rumi possessed the passionate heart that I long for.

Rumi's awakening to "passion's cup" and the beauty of God came when he met a wild, wandering dervish named Shams Tabrizi (the Sun of Tabriz).

Before meeting Shams, Rumi's family had moved to what is now Konya, Turkey, because of political instability and the threat of invasion by the Mongols. This city, the ancient Iconium, was also known as Rum, from which Rumi took his name. Rumi's father became a distinguished scholar at the university in Konya and when he died, Rumi took his place.

Rumi gained fame and respect, and people from all over the world came to hear him teach. Then one day, Shams appeared. Shams had been looking his entire life for the "perfect student," one with whom he could share a deep spiritual rapport. When he was in his sixties, Shams finally found this student in Rumi. Several versions of the meeting have circulated, but my favorite is the one told by Mojdeh Bayat and Mohammad Ali Jamnia in *Tales from the Land of the Sufis.*

One day Rumi sat teaching a group of students when suddenly Shams walked in, pointed to a stack of books, and asked Rumi, "What are these?" Rumi, thinking Shams a shabby beggar, replied that he wouldn't understand. Suddenly, fire shot from the books and Rumi, alarmed, asked what was happening. "Nor would you understand this," said Shams. With that, Rumi gave up his teaching post to follow Shams and enter more deeply into the mysteries of God.

Though Rumi was a spiritual man before he met Shams, Rumi saw in Shams a spiritual reality that he had not previously glimpsed. Having spent his life immersed in books and academic teaching, Rumi suddenly realized that though study had accomplished much in his life, it was time to go beyond study, into the realm of pure spirit, seeking divine union with God.

This idea of "going beyond the intellect" is also illustrated in a story of the Great Maggid, the successor to the founder of the mystical branch of Judaism—Hasidism. Author and Rabbi Marc Gafni tells the story:

> It is said that the Great Maggid would convene his inner circle every night to teach [his disciples] the sacred texts. All of his greatest students would gather. When the Maggid would begin to speak "And God said . . ." Reb Zushya would leap up, overwhelmed with desire. He would yell out, "And God said! God said!" He would spin around and around like a leaf in the wind, and then faint, unconscious for the rest of the teaching. Every night it was the same thing. The other disciples would tease him, saying, "Zushya, you're missing all the holy teachings!" This teasing

went on for days and days until finally the master said, "Leave him alone; he's the only one who gets it."

Another example of going beyond the intellect, also from Judaism, explains why Adam and Eve were forbidden to eat from the tree of knowledge of good and evil. Why was eating from this tree a sin? Jewish mystics tell us that prior to obtaining this intellectual knowledge, humankind enjoyed purity and innocence, and thus, a perfect relationship with God.

Within the Christian tradition, the apostle Paul echoes this when he tells us that knowledge of the law brought about a kind of spiritual death. Though Christians may interpret this spiritual death as "original sin," it can also be seen through the Jewish mystics' eyes—that an intellectual knowledge of good and evil robbed humankind of its innocence and pure relationship with God. The mystic's goal, then, is to "return" to this pure state of being in the heart, which I'll talk about in a later chapter.

The emphasis upon the heart greatly attracted the well-known Catholic mystic, Thomas Merton. In a speech to a group of Catholic Sisters in Alaska, Merton said, "The heart is the faculty by which man knows God. . . . The Sufis have ways of learning to pray so that you are really praying in the heart, from the heart, [and] not just saying words, just thinking good thoughts or making intentions."

"The heart," writes author Laleh Bakhtiar, Ph.D, "is the *seat of consciousness of God and is capable of progressing the self towards perfection.*"

A Hasidic rabbi with whom I studied weekly for several years once said this: "There is no fight between the heart and the intellect. The fight is between spirituality and materialism."

Bayat and Jamnia tell a lovely story of a poor shepherd with a pure heart who, like David, basked in a close communion with God as he tended his flock.

Then one day, Moses came by and heard what he took to be a blasphemous prayer. The shepherd's prayer was one of longing to sew God's clothes, mend God's socks, comb God's hair, and bring God milk.

Moses reprimanded the shepherd, calling his prayer outrageous and insulting to God. God isn't a human being, Moses said, that he wears clothes and drinks milk.

The shepherd, who recognized Moses as a prophet of God, turned away in shame, left his flock, and traveled to the desert. Shortly thereafter God spoke to Moses and said, "Remember that in Love, words are only the outer husk and mean nothing. We pay no heed to the beauty of the phrase or the composition of the sentence. We look only at the inner condition of the heart. . . . In that way We know the sincerity of Our creatures, even though their words may be artless. For those who burn with Love have burned their words as well."

Moses, in his supreme humility, listened in awe and ran off immediately to apologize to the shepherd. After searching for many days, he found the shepherd, his clothes torn and disheveled. Kneeling beside him, Moses confessed that God didn't require "etiquette" in prayer, and that he was free to speak to God in any way he pleased.

The shepherd, however, had passed the stage of words, his heart now simply illuminated with God's presence.

This is the heart of the mystic, the heart that the apostle Paul in the Greek Testament says prays with "sighs too deep for words." "The pure in heart," said Jesus, "will see God," and these words are echoed in the beliefs of the Sufis, who see the heart as a mirror that, when polished by continual remembrance of God, reflects God. The deepest desire and goal of the mystic is simply to "see" God with the heart.

. . . .

Each Wednesday afternoon I visit the homebound of my church. At least half of the people I regularly visit have Alzheimer's or dementia, yet almost every week, I'm reminded that when the mind disintegrates, the heart can continue to shine through. Last week, for instance, I visited a woman who is in the final stages of Alzheimer's. She no longer recognizes anyone, can't communicate, and her arms are wrapped in cloth to prevent her from scratching wounds onto her skin.

Mrs. Jameson's mind has retained only a few sentences, which she seems to communicate with sincerity and knowledge of what she's saying: "You're so sweet. You're so pretty. You're so kind. You're such sunshine." I recently e-mailed our associate pastor, Preston Bright, who's the liaison for my committee, about my visit with Mrs. Jameson. "I find it amazing," I wrote him, "that the few words she's retained are beautiful words of affirmation."

Mrs. Jameson also loves to sing. Though she doesn't remember any words to the songs, a soft tremolo floats from her. "La laaaa la la laaaa," she hums, gripping my hand, a continual smile illuminating her face.

Another woman I used to visit, Opal Wortham, also in the final stages of Alzheimer's, finally reached a point where she could no longer communicate and seemed to recognize no one except her daughter, Norma Lee. Despite these circumstances, Mrs. Wortham continued to do little things for the other Alzheimer's victims with whom she lived.

Often, she'd wheel herself over to straighten another woman's dress. If someone passed by her, Mrs. Wortham would reach out to tenderly touch them. One day when I arrived, she frantically latched onto me and pulled me down the hall, one hand rolling her wheelchair, the other hand clinging to me. Pulling me into a

room, Mrs. Wortham pointed to a woman who had fallen out of
bed and was lying on the floor.

While these women have naturally open hearts, the rest of us
have to cultivate practices that help us break open our hearts both
to God and to others. For me, this is gradually coming through
both a daily time of meditation and through a weekly meeting with
a few dervishes. Thus, each week, after my afternoon visits with
the homebound, I have dinner, then drive to Wahhaba's for *zikr*.

Usually I arrive a little early and sit on the couch talking to
Wahhaba as she lights candles. Pictures of Sufi masters fill the surface
area of her piano. Wahhaba's voice and demeanor are soft, and she
exudes a continual undercurrent of excitement about spirituality.

As people arrive, we chat a bit, then sit in a circle with our
eyes closed, breathing and emptying our minds of the worries and
busyness of the day. Wahhaba then begins *sohbet*, her voice barely
rising above a whisper. Wahhaba listens carefully to her heart as
she speaks, remaining open to whatever message she feels one of
us might need at the moment.

Some weeks she reads a story or passage from a book by a Sufi
master, and we listen with our eyes closed, savoring the lesson.
Closing our eyes not only helps block out distractions, it also,
more importantly, allows us to focus deeply within, hearing the
whisperings of God within our hearts.

After *sohbet*, Wahhaba explains the particular *zikr* for the
evening. Certain chants have been basic to Sufi practice for hundreds
of years. Virtually all orders focus their *zikrs* on the ninety-nine
Divine Names of God, as well as on a couple of key phrases.
Chanting a particular Name is supposed to evoke that particular
attribute of God within one's own heart and within the world
around us. For me, it's also a form of worship. One of these, *La
ilaha illa 'llah*, has a powerful effect upon me each time I repeat it.

The first time I chanted this phrase was at the Caravan of the Beautiful, the retreat I attended in Austin. At the end of the weekend, as I drove back to Dallas, this phrase continued to reverberate in my heart and mind. Even though we had chanted dozens of Names and phrases, this was the only one I remembered, and since I didn't have any idea what it meant, I called Wahhaba when I got home. Sufis believe the heart often registers an important message from God even when the intellect hasn't picked it up as significant, so I was startled when she told me that the phrase means, "There is no God but God."

This phrase is closely related to Judaism's most important prayer, the *Shema: Shema Israel, Adonai Ehloheinu, Adonai Echod.* Hear, O Israel! The Lord our God, the Lord is One. I love this prayer not only because it holds such an important place in a religion I've come to love, but also because it's a prayer that emphasizes that only one God exists and that this God is the God of everything and everyone. So at Wahhaba's this evening, one of the phrases happens to be the one I love most: *La ilaha illa 'llah.* Wahhaba's *zikrs* have the temperament of Buddhist chants: very slow and intentional. Moving our heads to the left, we chant, *La.* Then to the right: *Ilaha.* Bowing our heads: *illa.* Then looking towards the heavens: *llaaaahhhh.* As we slowly breathe the last syllable, I'm inexplicably filled with the still, quiet presence of God.

When I first began participating in *zikr* with the little group at Wahhaba's, I was self-conscious, often opening my eyes to see what others were doing. Gradually, though, I began to move into the recesses of my heart, losing awareness of all but God. Of course, I never do this perfectly, but there have been times that I feel the melting of my heart into God so intensely that I carry a powerful sense of God's presence with me for days.

Though the Sufi *zikr* may seem strange to newcomers, its goal is simply to clear the mind and open the heart so that a still, quiet place within opens, and we can hear the eternal voice of God. For the Sufi, this place is the inner recess of the heart—the dwelling place of God.

Thomas Merton, who had, before his death, planned a trip to visit a close Sufi friend in Pakistan, wrote this:

"At the center of our being is a point of nothingness which is untouched by sin and illusion, a point of pure truth, a point or spark which belongs entirely to God. . . . This little point . . . is the pure glory of God in us. . . . It is like a pure diamond, blazing with the invisible light of heaven."

Most spiritual or religious groups who use meditation have their own special chant. Not long ago, for instance, I watched a group of Tantric monks from Tibet create a sand mandala. During the opening and closing ceremonies, they uttered a guttural chant that is unique to their sect of Buddhism. "If the Himalayas sang," a monk said during another ceremony in what I took to be a quote from another source, "their melody would be the chant of the Tibetan monks."

The chants that Sufis do most often—the ninety-nine Most Beautiful Names of God, recited with symbolic movements and rhythmic breathing—awaken particular qualities within one's heart. For instance, I long to move to an area of the country that's mountainous, because I find that terrain so spiritually invigorating. Because of this love, I've begun meditating on the Divine Names *al-Jalil* and *al-Wasi*: the Majestic and the Vast.

Sufism has taught me that the intense feelings which the mountains arouse in me are just that: *in me.* The longing I feel for the tangible beauty of the mountains is in reality a much deeper longing: my soul's cry for God. By meditating on the divine attributes of majesty and vastness, I bring to my heart the Majesty and Vastness of God, even while living in a geographical location that leaves me uninspired.

When I was involved with a Jewish Renewal group, Hesha Abrams, the student rabbi who led the group, once gave us a meditation based on various Hebrew Names or attributes of God: *Adonai* (Ineffable One), *Shalom* (Peace), *Ribbono Shel Olam* (Master of the Universe), and *HaRachaman* (Merciful One).

Jews sometimes pray to God by invoking the name that best conveys their prayer. Hebrew has many names for God—*El Olam*, *YHVH*, and *El Ro'i* represent a few of them, and each evokes a different quality. Praying to God merely with the name *God* can lock us into a single image, whereas praying to different names can instill a sense of God's multifaceted nature.

In some Sufi groups, we chant the Names (usually two during a single *zikr*) a set number of times, using prayer beads. Anyone in any religion, including Christianity, that uses chant will tell you that this is far from "vain repetition." Each time the Name is spoken, it penetrates a bit more deeply. Soon, awareness of one's self begins to diminish, replaced by a deeper awareness of God. The heart gradually opens, becoming increasingly aware of and attuned to the voice and presence of God.

Zikr has had lasting effects on both my personality and my spirituality. The quiet place where I find God has become more easily accessible throughout the day. When I'm stressed, hurt or confused, I can more readily sense God's calming Presence within. My emotions don't disappear, but much of the time, they don't have the same power over me.

The goal of *zikr* is beautifully illustrated in a story about the great Sufi sheikh Abu Sa'id. One day, someone told the sheikh that he'd seen someone walking on water. The sheikh wasn't impressed, telling the man that a frog and mosquito can walk on water.

The sheikh also was nonplussed by a tale of a man who could fly, pointing out that birds fly. When the man told the sheikh about someone who could mystically transport himself from one geographical area to another, the sheikh retorted that even Satan could do that. Don't look at these things as signs of spirituality, the sheikh said. Look at those who can be in any situation without forgetting God for a single moment.

Such *remembrance* of God is not an intellectual remembrance. It's a remembrance that reverberates in the heart, even while the intellect is engaged with study, conversation, or work. Most Christians will readily recognize in this the example of Brother Lawrence, author of the classic *The Practice of the Presence of God*.

In a letter to one of his friends, Brother Lawrence once wrote, "If I were to be responsible for guiding souls in the right direction, I would urge everyone to be aware of God's constant presence, if for no other reason than because his presence is a delight to our souls and spirits." This great saint felt the intimate presence of God every moment and in every task of life, including the most mundane.

There's a lovely midrash (biblical commentary) in Judaism which says that the holy words of Torah should "sit" upon your heart so that when it opens, the words will "fall in." This is the goal of *zikr*. We can't force our hearts to open. But as we invoke the Names of God, the debris that clutters the vast chasm of our hearts is swept clean, and the beauty and splendor of God fill the space that we're clearing. The words "fall in" and gradually, with each breath we take, we "remember" God. It is then that we realize that before we even had breath, and long after we've ceased to breathe on this earth, God eternally remembers us. From God we came, and to God, by his grace, we are returning.

CHAPTER FOUR

Becoming Love

*R*isa Ranch in the hill country of Texas: I'm here for the fourth year in a row, along with dozens of others, sitting on a small pile of throw rugs, and inhaling deeply the spring breeze that drifts across the creek and gently undulates the limbs of the trees. *Sohbet* is about to begin and Shahabuddin asks us the following question:

"What is your secret?"

"My secret has to do with the things I've not accepted about myself," says Alec Tahmassebi.

"My secret is that I'd like to stop being a mystery to myself," responds another man.

"Mine," I say, "is that I'm discovering I'm not who I always thought I was."

Everyone shares an answer, and I notice that many of our secrets are about our own self-discovery. Sufism is a mystical path that demands brutal honesty in self-analysis. God's light can only shine on us and purify us when we admit our shortcomings. This is a process that's far more difficult than most imagine. Often, it's the reason that people who have begun traveling this difficult, spiritual path turn back or remain at an elementary level.

As I've begun my own journey, with a great deal of fear and trepidation as well as joy, I've discovered that the more honest I am with myself, the freer I am to love others. "Why do you see the speck in your neighbor's eye, but do not notice the log in your own eye?" Jesus asked.

Since I've been traveling the Sufi path, many passages in Scripture, such as this one in Matthew, have jumped out at me in ways they had never done before. Jesus was telling me that I'm the one that I need to work on, and I'm finding that I can better obey his message of love when I'm honest about my own shortcomings and more forgiving of the failures of others.

People in the group continue to share their "secrets" and then, as everyone grows quiet, my friend Wahhaba suddenly stands and begins walking around the room. She hasn't shared her secret, but she's about to share it in a nonverbal way: by looking quietly and deeply into each of our eyes.

During spiritual exercises or rituals, my teachers in both Judaism and Sufism have often instructed us to look into one another's eyes. They teach that when you look into someone's eyes, you're not merely looking at the organ of sight, you're looking into the soul. You're seeing God in the eyes of another person. An extraordinary connection of divine love arises. Wahhaba takes probably fifteen minutes to complete the circle, but no one is uneasy, including the teachers. Wahhaba moves slowly, taking her time with each and every person present, occasionally reaching up to caress someone's face, but usually, just looking into our eyes. Several of us, including myself, begin weeping.

....

For the Sufi, love is the path to God. Rumi tells us that only the person whose garment is "rent by the violence of love" can be wholly pure from covetousness and sin. Hazrat Inayat Khan, the Indian master who brought Sufism to the West, reminds us that love makes the heart sincere. When we love from the heart, we can't lie or effectively put on masks. We simply love unconditionally, deeply, and without reservation. Love strips away the masks we wear.

This fiery love is thoroughly divine, originating from God, who sets the heart ablaze with single-focused adoration. "The fire of love burns so intensely . . . that everything but God is consumed." writes one Sufi, and another, Abu Sa'id, compares the lover of God to the full moon, "which has no light of its own but fully reflects that of the glorious sun (God)."

The Bible depicts a love full of intense feeling. The portrayal of God by the Hebrew prophets has attracted me for as long as I can remember. Growing up, I loved reading about a God who would stop at nothing to win the hearts of those whom he loved.

As I grew older, however, I sometimes heard ministers and teachers denigrate the passionate side of love. One guest minister recently told our congregation that the "feeling" of love might very well just be indigestion!

Yet as I began to study the biblical concept of love, what I found astounded me. The traditional definition of love in Christianity springs from a mistaken view of the four Greek words for love: *agape, philia, storge,* and *eros.*

The popular idea that these words represent different kinds of love is mistaken. In reality, the ancient Greeks used the word *agape* merely as a greeting of welcome and not as a *kind* of love at all. Likewise, *philia* expressed many kinds of love, not just "friendship" love. The Greeks used it as a suffix or prefix, attached to a root word which implied a deep love for something, such as *philosophon* (love of wisdom), or *philomachos* (love of fighting). This is precisely the way we use *philo* in English, as a prefix or suffix meaning a passionate love of something: *bibliophile* (intense lover of books), *philologue* (lover of words), and *philanthropist* (love of humankind).

Though the writers of the Greek Testament chose a new word to express love—*agape*—this word, like *eros*, expresses more than one kind of love. It is used to express the same wide range of loves that our English word expresses. In the Greek Testament, for instance, *agape* indicates the love of important seats in the synagogue, love of life, love of the world (in a negative sense), and love of God. In the Septuagint—the Greek translation of the Hebrew Testament—*agape* is used to describe Amnon's love for Tamar, his half-sister whom he raped and subsequently despised. It's also used throughout the Song of Songs to express sexual love, and the psalmist uses it to warn against love of vanity.

The problem with the traditional interpretation of *agape* is that it's often pitted against *eros* and thus can be robbed of its passion. The love depicted throughout the Bible—both Testaments—is a love that demands a passion of the heart, soul, and mind. Rather than getting caught up in the supposedly different meanings of love expressed in Greek, we'd do much better looking at the way love is *described* in Scripture.

The Hebrew prophets speak of an intensely felt love that consumes one with longing, and David sings of love as only a troubadour can, with romance and passion. Jesus echoes the Hebraic *Shema*, telling us to love with every aspect of our being; the apostle Paul speaks of a love filled with joy and longing; and the apostle Peter tells us to love deeply and sincerely, from the heart.

Love, for the Sufi, as for the majority of mystics in all religions, is passion and fire. "Be drunk on Love," writes Rumi, "for only Love exists. At every instant Love calls from near and far."

And again, "Love is the endless ocean of God."

Shams-ud-din Muhammad Hafiz, another well-known Sufi poet, tells us that love in Sufism is the supreme path to God. "The subject tonight is Love," he writes, "and for tomorrow night as well. As a matter of fact, I know of no better topic for us to discuss until we all die!"

John Michael Talbot, the Franciscan musician and author, finds himself able to live the radical, simple life of Jesus when he meditates on God as a fire, allowing God to inflame his entire life.

Because of the passion and fire in romantic love, most mystics use sensual terminology to compare the relationship between God and humankind. Sufis write of the lover being intoxicated with longing for the Beloved. The kabbalistic texts of Judaism, such as the *Zohar*, are rife with such terminology, and of course, the biblical book, the Song of Songs, erotically depicts the longing and passion associated with intense, romantic love—a reflection of humankind's thirst for God and God's thirst for us. Many Christian mystics could think of no better allegory than the erotic to depict this divine, fiery relationship. St. Teresa of Avila, for instance, depicted her ecstatic encounters with God in terms of marriage, and had a vision in which Jesus presented her with a wedding ring. Her rapturous experiences were so intense that in one vision, she writes of an angel piercing her heart with a "large golden dart," which left her "on fire with the great love of God."

. . . .

Another aspect of love I feel drawn toward is *affection*, and many other Sufis appear to feel the same way. To some people, affection can seem superficial or unimportant, but to me, it's an integral aspect of love. I loved it when once, after *zikr*, Baba threw up his hands and called loudly, "Kiss! Kiss!"

Another time, at the conclusion of *sohbet*, Shahabuddin said, "Don't forget to hug one another—and make it juicy! Don't be *spiritual*."

Though these teachers would never condone inappropriate relationships, they grow tired, as do I, of being self-conscious or overly wary in our displays of affection toward one another.

One of my favorite stories of St. Francis shows the emphasis he placed on affection. One day Francis was riding through the outskirts of Assisi when he met a leper. Francis abhorred lepers, recoiling from the sight of them, and even though this particular day was no exception, he slowly dismounted from his horse. Full of fear and horror, Francis approached the leper and embraced him. When the man held out his hands to receive money, Francis first kissed his hands, then filled them with money. After that day, Francis went out purposely to find lepers and help them, always "kiss[ing] their hands and their faces . . . with affectionate compassion."

Not long ago I was reminded of this story when I went to visit a friend who has impaired intellectual ability and was also ill with a serious viral infection. I had brought her a Christmas present, a ceramic snowman filled with candy, and she repeatedly asked me to hold it close to her face so she could see it.

"Oh, it's so cute!" she said. "Let me see it again! Oh, it's so cute!"

After I had showed it to her for about the tenth time, she suddenly said, "Give me a kiss!"

I was repulsed. Her eyes were crusted over and oozing with fluid. "The flu's going around, girl," I tried to say, lightly. "I don't want to get sick!" The smile faded from her face and her eyes filled with hurt and pain. Shame gripped my heart, but I still couldn't bring myself to kiss her. What a gift St. Francis gave to the leper,

I thought as I left my friend, unwilling to offer her the affection that she needed. We can denigrate the place of affection in love all we want, but the reality is people feel loved through touch and tender, personal contact.

············

Inseparable from love is *longing*, a recurrent theme in Sufi stories and teaching. God is always present with us, yet we long for a more intimate, more powerful, and more tangible feeling of that presence. "My spirit faints with longing," cries the psalmist, and the seventh-century saint, Maximos the Confessor, the love-inflamed martyr for God, writes of an "intense longing for God" in which the "intellect rises above the realm of created beings."

Sufis, as well as many other mystics, believe that longing in and of itself is a connection with God. In one story, the Sufis tell of a devoted man who cried out all day to God: "Allah! Allah!"

Then one day a cynic appeared and said to the man, "So! I have heard you calling out, but have you ever gotten any response?"

The man had no answer, and so he quit praying. That evening Khidr, the mysterious divine guide who sometimes appears to sincere Sufi seekers, came to the man and asked him why he had stopped praying.

"Because I've never heard anything back!" the man said.

Khidr replied: "The longing you express is the return message. The grief you cry out from draws you toward union. Your pure sadness that wants help is the secret cup. Listen to the moan of a dog for its master. That whining *is* the connection."

Often pain jolts us from the petty concerns of everyday life and causes us to cry out to God. Longing is painful, but when it's filled with hope and anticipation, we don't want to be rid of it. We

long for God with the eager anticipation of fulfillment, even if for
brief moments at a time. Since God is always present and available,
it's our longing that drives us to cry out for and recognize that
Presence.

Rumi wrote all of his most beautiful poetry after his second and
final separation from his beloved Shams—his spiritual awakener—
repeatedly stating that though his longing was filled with pain, it
filled him with delight, for it drove him towards union with God.

> Though I am
> in this
> hell and fire,
> I'm filled with
> honey and nectar. . . .

Elsewhere Rumi writes,

> If your mind and stomach
> burn with the fire of hunger
> it will be like a heavenly song for your heart.
> In each moment that fire rages
> it will burn away a hundred veils
> and carry you a thousand steps
> toward your goal.

Because most of us only get a taste or glimpse now and then of
the full, ecstatic union with God that mystics write about, and
because the journey to get there is long and filled with challenges,
we derive pleasure in the very longing that drives us. Rabbi Marc
Gafni writes that "longing and desire are good not because . . . all of
our yearning will be fulfilled or realized, but because yearning itself
fulfills us." Desire, he writes, fills us with life and allows us to touch
fulfillment, even when we don't experience it in its entirety.

Those who find satisfaction and happiness in their spiritual seeking are those who have learned to enjoy the *process* and to relish the moments, however rare, of pure, blissful contact with God. In one of Deepak Chopra's imaginative and humorous stories about the legendary King Arthur as a child, learning about life and God from the wizard Merlin, Chopra depicts Arthur struggling with the seeming indifference of God. "If God isn't indifferent," Arthur asks, "then why doesn't he show his intentions?"

"Ah," Merlin says, "you must search to find that out. Perhaps this whole world was intended as a game of divine hide-and-seek."

"Then it would be a very cruel game," Arthur protests.

Merlin then pushes Arthur to think more deeply about God. When God seems far away, Merlin says, it's because we've sent him away. We've become caught up in our often petty angers and frustrations, set our hearts on material possessions, or simply become too filled with ourselves to hear the whispers of God. Messages, Merlin tells Arthur, "remain disguised so long as our perception is clouded." When this happens, he continues, a mysterious clue, a divine act, that is wholly loving can seem to be the work of an indifferent God.

This lesson is echoed in Rumi's poetry about God.

What disguises he wears,
what tricks he invents!
If he appears in one shape, as spirit he slips the snare.
When you seek him above, he shines like the moon in water;
when you enter the water he flees skyward.
When you seek him in the placeless, he guides you to place.
When you seek him in place, he guides you to the
placeless."

If you attempt to experience God in a single expression and encapsulate God in a single form, Rumi is saying, you'll find that God has burst from that expression and form and hidden elsewhere, beckoning us to come and look for God there. New aspects of God's nature are always awaiting our discovery, and part of the joy and excitement lies in our willingness to do the mysterious work of unveiling them.

"Do not despair if the Beloved pushes you away," writes Rumi. "If he pushes you away today it's only so he can draw you back tomorrow." Rumi, of course, knows that God doesn't literally push us away; rather, God beckons us to see God with new eyes and to experience God in diverse ways. God is adventurous, and when we embrace this truth, a great deal of joy and excitement leaps onto the path of our spiritual quest.

"Teacher, which commandment in the law is the greatest?" someone once asked Jesus. He replied, reiterating the beloved prayer of the Jews, "You shall love the Lord your God with all your heart, and with all your soul, and with all your mind." "This," Jesus said, "is the greatest and first commandment." Then, continuing to quote from the Hebrew Scripture, he added, "And a second is like it: 'You shall love your neighbor as yourself.' On these two commandments hang all the law and the prophets."

The apostle John repeated this time and time again: "God is love," he writes. "and those who abide in love abide in God, and God abides in him." Indeed, in his brief, first epistle, John uses a form of the word "love" an astonishing forty-five times.

Bayat and Jamnia show us the transforming power of longing and love through a story of a pious Sufi shaykh named San'an. This shaykh, who had lived for fifty years in a sanctuary teaching his dervishes the ways of purity in the Sufi path, dreamt one night that he had bowed to an idol. Each night the dream reoccurred, and the shaykh, utterly distressed, set out for Byzantium, along with some of his dervishes, to try and discover its meaning. When they arrived, the shaykh heard a beautiful voice, a woman singing a love song, that made his "heart bleed with desire." When he saw the woman, he became so absorbed that he couldn't move from the spot beside her window. He forgot who he was and where he had come from. But though he wept and wailed beneath her window, she went about her business as if unaware of his presence.

The shaykh crawled in the dirt, "soaking it with his tears." The nights had never seemed so endless to him, and though he'd experienced intense pain in his life, nothing had ever been so agonizing.

When the dervishes begged him to perform the ritual for cleansing the soul, the shaykh asked them how they could even speak of ablution when they obviously knew nothing about the pain of love.

The dervishes pleaded with their shaykh to repent, but he simply replied that he had repented, but only of his shaykh-hood. The only regret he held was that he hadn't fallen in love sooner.

The shaykh stopped at nothing to win his beloved. He found a spot beside a road where she traveled, and he ate crumbs tossed to the dogs, just to glimpse her beauty. When he was asked to prove his love by wallowing with the pigs, he didn't hesitate. Most of his dervishes eventually despaired and left him. When they arrived back home a holy man reprimanded them for abandoning their teacher, so they returned—only to find him in a state of complete, divine bliss.

"Having passed beyond mosque and temple, . . . having lost all attachment to status or piety, [the shaykh] was free from self, united with his True Beloved. . . . his eyes shone with the secret joy known only to the Beloved and the lover." He had experienced the last stage of his long and holy journey—the annihilation of everything except his consciousness of and love for God.

For the Sufi, and for all seekers of God, this is the goal: to be filled gradually, moment by moment, with a sense of the divine presence, until nothing but God remains. The journey is long and arduous, but love drives us onward—a love that is passionate, consuming, and self-obliterating. With every breath we're given a new opportunity to deepen our quest, a broader capacity to experience God, and a more brimming desire to fully live the love we feel.

In a loose quotation of the prophet Isaiah, St. Paul writes that, "What no eye has seen, nor ear heard, nor the human heart conceived, what God has prepared for those who love him." Christians often assume Paul is writing here of the afterlife, but Paul makes it clear in the same sentence that he's referring to what *God has already made available*.

God has revealed these mysteries, Paul says, because the "Spirit searches everything, even the depths of God." Paul, the man who had life-altering visions, who spoke of mystical journeys to the "third" heaven, and who knew of the prayer that can only be uttered by "sighs too deep for words," had a heart's desire similar to a Sufi, for mystics, regardless of their religion or theology, have hearts united by one desire: a passion to experience God.

CHAPTER FIVE

From Goodness to Purity

*I*n a little town in Turkey—Hacıbektaş—in a sacred spot beside a large, hollow rock, I stood, along with Baba, Jem, and about forty dervishes from America, Canada, Turkey, Azerbaijan, and elsewhere. The town was named after a thirteenth-century saint named Hacı Bektaş known for his loving-kindness, his advocacy of education for women, his deep respect for science, and his inner purity, and he often entered this rock through a small passageway to find seclusion to meditate.

Several feet from the entryway, there's a very small exit hole, shaped in such a way that one can slide out of it only by positioning and moving the body in a particular manner. The dervishes lined up as Baba and his two adult sons climbed to the top of the rock to watch. For all of us, this afternoon formed a symbolic birthing ritual, similar to Christian baptism.

The first person scrunched over, entered the rock, and with Jem's encouragement and instruction, managed, after several twists and attempts, to wiggle through the tiny exit. Baba, dressed in western clothes and a warm Turkish cap, waved his cane above his head, his twinkle-eyed smile lighting up the overcast morning. "Natural childbirth!" he called out.

"No forceps needed!" When I snapped his picture, he grinned and said, "Thank you!"

One by one each dervish entered. A few of the younger and more athletic-looking men and women slid through easily. Others repeatedly had trouble. When this happened, Baba called to Jem: "Problems with the childbirth! Forceps needed!"

One woman gave up after several attempts, but Jem comforted and encouraged her and she finally emerged, bursting into tears as she did so. Everyone made it through, though it took most several tries, re-twisting their bodies until they found the needed position. Most emerged with a glow of happiness on their faces.

Birthing rituals have been common among virtually all religions, in all cultures, in every place in the world. They are symbols of new life, change, and fresh starts. We enter the spiritual womb and emerge, spiritually charged and ready to face the challenges of life with renewed excitement, hope, and a sense of promise. Jesus speaks of being "born again," first of water (our physical birth), then of the Spirit.

During the past ten years or so, I've experienced numerous rebirths in my life—deepening and expanding my spiritual life— and have had dreams and visions which pointed me in new directions and helped me see life and God in new ways. One of the most recent and powerful of these rebirths, or "awakenings," has been a more intense desire for inner purity.

Until the last decade, living by a moral code was the "spirituality" in my life. I placed great emphasis on aspects of morality that were tangible—clear laws by which I could measure my own "goodness." I discovered that I had an innate need within myself for rigidity, which was reinforced by the teachings of some of the churches I attended.

As a teenager, I had been the epitome of the rebellion of the seventies. Yet I often came home and wrote in my diary of my disgust and frustration with myself. *Tomorrow I'm going to start being good,* I'd write, and then I'd fill my head with a list of what that meant—unfailingly sentencing myself to failure. I'd never smoke again, I'd decide. I'd stop going out with my friends to parties, stop telling lies, and give up drugs. I'd trade my faded, tattered blue jeans for a pretty skirt, like the "good" girls at church wore (they constituted my definition of goodness), talk in a softer, kinder manner, and stop swearing. I'd even mimic the way the good girls walked and sat and acted in class.

While this level of goodness seemed incredibly difficult at the time, it is, in reality, actually attainable *simply because it's outward and measurable.* It wasn't until my mid-thirties that I realized that what I had called morality was mostly an outward veneer and a good deal of it had nothing to do with goodness at all.

Amazingly, however, it took another full decade before the concept of inner purity, and my deep longing for it, began to take hold of me. St. Teresa of Avila first awakened this understanding and desire, but Sufism plunged me headlong onto the path.

· · · · · · · ·

Sufis place great emphasis on inner purity. At each new level of spiritual progress, the Sufis believe, one will become more humble and less jealous, more patient and less greedy, more compassionate and less contentious, more gentle and less self-deluded. In his *Degrees of the Soul,* Shaykh abd al-Khaliq al-Shabrawi lists and discusses numerous qualities of purity, and then reminds us that these make up only a small number of the qualities we should build in ourselves.

This kind of goodness is one that we work toward our entire lives. It is not a morality that is satisfied by giving up a few outward "sins" each week. We don't check these qualities off on a list of good things we've achieved. In fact, as our purity increases, we're *less* aware of it! "If you were to be in a state of sincerity," writes one Sufi master, "you would not think of yourself as being in a state of sincerity!"

This level of purity is illustrated in the story of a king who came to a Sufi master declaring his desire to give up his royal position and to take up the life of a humble servant. The *murshid*, or Sufi master, told the king he would accept him on "probation" and gave him the daily task of taking the trash to the city dump.

After many months, the dervishes began to pity the former king and went to their teacher, asking that the man be accepted and initiated as a student. The teacher replied that the man was not yet ready. One dervish persisted and so the teacher permitted him to test the former king in any way he chose, and to report the results to the teacher.

The next day the dervish hid alongside the path that the former king took on his way to the trash heap. When the dervish saw the former king approaching, he leaped from his hiding spot, purposefully bumped into him, and caused the trash to spill. "Had I still been a king as I was," the man said to the dervish, "I would have responded as a king. But now, of course, I am not, so I must not show my temper." Then he gathered the trash and went on his way.

The dervish reported back to his *murshid*, who replied, "Did I not tell you he is not ready?"

So the dervish waited again for the man, and once again threw himself in front of him, causing him to spill the trash. This time, the former king looked at the dervish and without a word, picked up the trash and carried it to the town dump. The dervish reported the result of the test, and the *murshid* said, "Not ready. Not ready."

A third time the dervish purposely leaped in front of the man and caused him to spill the trash. This time the former king didn't even look at the dervish. He simply picked up the trash and took it to the dump. After this, the *murshid* accepted him into the ranks of the dervishes, initiating him into the mystical path of Sufism. The former king had gone beyond restraint, beyond conscious effort toward having a pure heart, and had entered into a realm in which one is not even conscious of insult. This, for the Sufi, is genuine purity.

When I think about Shaykh al-Shabrawi's vision of purity, I sense something of what the prophet Isaiah must have felt when he encountered the glory and holiness of God, and realized that his human righteousness, in comparison, was as "filthy rags." This doesn't reflect on our value or worth, nor is it even a statement about the basic nature of humankind; rather, it shows that purity is far more than what I envisioned and worked for as a teenager—a list of traits I could measure and check off in my efforts to be good.

Genuine purity goes much further than not lying, cheating, or stealing. The apostle Paul tells us that "the fruit of the Spirit is love, joy, peace, patience, kindness, generosity, faithfulness, gentleness, and self-control."

Elsewhere, Paul tells us to think about things that are true, honorable, just, pure, pleasing, commendable, excellent, and praiseworthy. "Thinking about these things" has meant, to me, an effort to be aware throughout the day of how I act and think, to notice how frequently negative emotions creep up and begin to control me, and then to consciously open myself up to God's forgiving and purifying Spirit.

This kind of inner purity involves, in Shaykh al-Shabrawi's words, being aware of our arrogance, pride, love of power, and envy. It demands that we reflect on the illusions we create about ourselves. It asks that we try to create peace among people, to yearn for and rely upon God, to be content, to acquire compassion for all creatures, to grieve over our failures, and to open our hearts in awe as we gaze upon the Divine.

We don't acquire these qualities by our own human effort, nor can they be merely outward actions, noble as those actions may be. Rather, we become more holy when we open our hearts to God and let God's glory, love, and holiness fill us. For me, this is precisely what zikr is all about. As I repeat the Divine Names of God, which represent God's attributes, I intentionally allow myself to be transformed in the deepest part of my being.

For most of us, this is a lifelong process, and each day is a precious opportunity to become increasingly full of kindness and love, ready to give to all who ask, and turning the other cheek without even an awareness that we are doing so.

· · · · · · · · ·

I have several meditations that I focus on throughout the day. One of my favorites is what a Turkish translator calls in a quaint English rendition, which I love: the "Seven Advice of Mevlana [Rumi]." I have several reminders hanging in different rooms of my home, all of which I bought at Rumi's tomb in Konya, Turkey. In my office hangs a fringed prayer mat that I've framed; the so-named "Advice" sits below a famous depiction of the saint, seated and bowed in prayer. Two whirling dervishes float in the margins, dressed in the traditional flowing, white robes of the Mevlevi dervishes (the order that Rumi's followers created). Intricate, colorful designs surround the dervishes. Another framed version hangs in another room so that each morning, before I begin my day, I'm reminded to choose one of Rumi's seven pieces of advice—one for each day of the week—to meditate upon throughout that day.

Rumi's Advice reflects the high level of inner purity that Sufis strive for. Here is the translation that hangs on my own wall:

> In generosity and helping others be like a river.
> In compassion and grace be like sun.
> In concealing others' faults be like night.
> In anger and fury be like dead.
> In modesty and humility be like earth.
> In tolerance be like a sea.
> Either exist as you are or be as you look.

Some days, I'll couple my particular "Rumi" meditation for that day with a *zikr* connected to the corresponding divine Name of God. (This is a personal practice and not characteristic of Sufi practice in general.) On the day I meditate on Rumi's advice to "be like night in concealing others' faults," for instance, I might chant the Name *al-Ghafur* (Concealer of Faults), along with the closely related Name *al-Ghaffar* (The Forgiver). A tiny prayer mat with a picture of Rumi sits beside me while I pray.

My meditations, of course, also show me just how far I have to go—a realization that, in Sufism, is the first step towards purity. The Sufis teach that we have to be courageous enough to face our shortcomings—to see ourselves as we really are—before we can become the person God wants us to be. If we're serious about pursuing purity, this task is agonizing and ego-shattering.

One Wednesday, for instance, I had been meditating on Rumi's advice to "be like dead in anger and fury." That morning, I'd driven, as I do most days, to a serene nature center near my home to take a walk. About two minutes into the walk I stubbed my toe on a rock and swore in anger at the rock. A few minutes earlier, when I first had driven into the parking lot, I had been mildly annoyed at all the cars parked there. That meant I probably wouldn't have "my" trail to myself, as I often did. Then, as I walked, I could hear people talking loudly, and I felt another mild flare-up. *Do these people not know that this place of great natural beauty demands quiet and reflection*, I wondered in irritation.

On and on it went. I got tired and felt annoyed that I'd chosen a trail too long for my energy level this particular day. I got mad at the *trail* for this. I inwardly complained about it being seventy-five degrees on the last day of December. I live in such a stupid, hot, and ugly state, I fumed. I was now mad at Texas. My legs and feet began to hurt, and I bitched to myself about growing older; I'd probably have to take some ibuprofen after this walk, which ticked me off at the aging process. All of this happened in the space of a single hour in a place where I typically find my greatest tranquility and least amount of stress!

That these were all minor annoyances didn't really matter. In fact, it demonstrates that an endless, often negative, flow of chatter goes on in most of our heads all day. Rumi said, "In anger and fury be like dead!" Obviously, this level of purity takes consistent and persistent opening of our hearts to God on a moment-to-moment basis. I have *so* far to go.

Yet—and this is the great joy—I'm actually becoming *aware* of these things! I'm recognizing the need for a radical change in my life in many areas. I have noticed how often I shade the truth, how frequently I wear masks and portray myself in less-than-honest ways instead of offering to others the gift of my true self ("appear as you are," says Rumi). I've begun to notice the negative, destructive words that spring so easily from my mouth (and thus, from my heart, as Jesus said), and the anger that can erupt from the smallest upsets.

On the other hand, I find myself listening to others more deeply, becoming less selfish with my time when someone needs me, and more easily getting through my emotions when circumstances upset my life and plans.

Surprisingly, I'm also, for the first time in my life, beginning to truly appreciate the concept of grace in the Judeo-Christian tradition. Some years back, I'd become angry over what I considered an abuse of this great doctrine of grace. In churches I have attended, people who appeared to me to be self-centered, unloving, and uninterested in spirituality were labeled children of God because of a single prayer they'd voiced, while people who lived lives of passionate spirituality and exhibited numerous qualities of purity were considered "unbelievers."

I don't want to imply here that all conservative Christians have a simplistic idea of sin and godliness. I know many Christians who do much soul searching, who don't abuse the concept of grace, and who strive to bring a meaningful level of spirituality to their daily lives. My own church community is one of the most vibrant, spiritual communities I've ever encountered, and many of the members consider themselves conservative. But by the time I'd reached my mid-thirties, I wasn't sure I wanted anything to do with the so-called Christian idea of grace.

Then, oddly, during my meditation times, during conferences unrelated to Christianity, and at other guided meditation sessions, I began to have recurring visions of Jesus. God, it seemed, was bringing me an important message. I began to reflect on the visions, and eventually felt that Jesus was wooing me to look at him in new ways, to reflect on the essence of his message, and most importantly, not to reject him because I had experienced a few people abusing his message.

I saw that one of the most important lessons Jesus delivered was that of authentic grace—a grace that doesn't take the place of agonizing spiritual work, that doesn't do away with a demand for holiness and purity, and that doesn't excuse us from taking on the tasks of social justice issues, caring for the poor, and taking up the fight to ensure equality and reasonable living conditions for people who aren't like us.

The grace that Jesus taught first of all had much to do with *offering it to others*. When someone insults us, for example, we shouldn't avenge ourselves, but rather we should respond graciously. When someone condemns another through gossip, or invasion of privacy, we should refuse to join in. When someone angers us, or hurts us, we should forgive. When a person uses poor judgment, we should help them, with mercy and encouragement, to live more wisely.

Jesus also taught that we should extend grace toward ourselves. While we're working to open our hearts to God's divine light, engaging in spiritual disciplines, learning what it means to always keep God in remembrance, struggling to drive out impurities from our hearts and replacing them with God's divine attributes, an awareness of God's grace is indispensable. Without it, we'd be utterly discouraged. We'd be filled with guilt by our failures, and our beautiful, joy-filled path towards God would become an austere, self-deprecating journey.

Not long ago my husband, Mike, and I spent an evening at an amusement park with our Iranian friends, Samira and Hassan, who had converted to Christianity shortly after arriving in the U.S. Samira and I, taking a break from the rides, bought some nachos and sat talking at a picnic table. Though Christianity certainly isn't the only religion that teaches God's grace and mercy, Samira had felt and understood this grace only after she became a Christian. It was, she told me, one of the greatest discoveries of her life.

As I listened to her, I felt her joy. She'd found, for the first time in her life, the deep knowledge that God loved her unconditionally.

Samira's words and enthusiasm seeped into my heart, and I thought again of how differently grace looks to someone who's lived without it. I sat quietly, knowing that I needed that fresh vision of grace myself, for as long as I'm on the journey towards purity, I'm going to fall and mess things up and have to start over, again and again. And I need God's mercy and grace and forgiveness when I do.

CHAPTER SIX

Tearing the Bandage Off: Dance

*L*ately I've been having dreams of being naked in public. Not the kind of dream where I'm giving a public speech and suddenly realize I don't have any clothes on, but ones in which I'm running and dancing with a wild, abandoned, exhilarating freedom.

The first time I had one of these dreams, I dreamt I was dancing through the mountains, sprinting up giant piles of boulders, jumping into streams, and splashing through them barefoot. Some of these mountains and streams careened through towns and, although no one was paying any attention to me, I became more and more self- conscious. Gradually, as I ran, I began to put my clothes back on.

In each dream I've had since that first one, I ceased being self-conscious and danced through the mountains with the freedom of a lifelong nudist. In one, a brilliant sunset appeared before me, and in another, I ran down from a peak to a pristine, secluded beach on the shores of the ocean. Without pause, I ran like a small child into the waves.

These dreams of transparent freedom represent for me the past ten years of my life, a time when I've been discovering a new level of spirituality. That began when I went to a new church where I found a heightened sense of love, acceptance, and freedom; it continued when I became involved in Judaism, where my vision of God expanded to include a Being of mystery and passion; and it's now also being deepened by Sufism, where I've begun to embrace a God beyond religious description—a God who dances and laughs and embraces every human being, regardless of his or her beliefs or religious affiliation. Such a God releases us to endlessly re-experience God in new and exciting ways.

For me, this has meant the freedom to find God in my own, personal way, rather than trying to conform to what's expected of me—spiritually—by others. For most of my life, I've not felt free. During my childhood, I longed to be like the "church kids." As an adult, I spent much of my life believing it dangerous to question anything I was taught. Even when I began to loosen my spiritual rigidity, I continued to fear judgment and criticism, trying continually to make myself acceptable to those who might be upset by the changes in my life.

I remember one morning in particular, not long after I'd left a church where I'd experienced a great deal of pain, my husband called to say that a friend wanted to stop by to "talk" to me. Mike wanted to know if it was OK if this friend came for lunch.

Immediately I began to wonder how I'd answer this friend's questions. I knew he would quote Bible verses and attempt to instill a sense of fear and guilt in me about my rejection of some of my prior beliefs. Panic seized me at the thought of this conversation, and I began shaking and crying. I still felt I needed to appease people with whom I no longer agreed, and this caused me a lot of anguish. I called Mike back and told him that I'd changed my mind and asked him not to bring the man home with him.

I still find myself hiding who I am in some ways and with some people, even though I'm now in my forties. Fortunately, however, that's changing. I still prefer not to spend my lunches with people who want to convince me that they hold *the Truth*, suggesting, somehow, that I do not, but I no longer have attacks of anxiety around them. My involvement with Sufism is helping me "take off my clothes" and risk spiritual transparency. In my dreams, I run and dance tirelessly through the mountains, surrounded by majestic, earthly beauty. In my life, I'm learning to run and dance with God, immersed in the beauty of the Divine.

············

Many Sufi orders incorporate either dance or symbolic movement into their *zikrs*. Samuel Lewis, who led the Sufi Ruhaniat International order before his death, and was affectionately known as "Sufi Sam" in the sixties, created many dances that are today known as Dances of Universal Peace. Lewis developed the dances by combining the Divine Names and phrases used in Sufi *zikrs* with folk dance movements from all over the world. He began doing this after receiving a series of dreams and visions.

A few months ago, Mike and I, along with a number of other people, ushered in the New Year with these dances. Around 8 PM, after gathering wood for the fire that would blaze in the middle of a giant tipi in a wooded area of Fort Worth, we shoved back the flap and ducked inside. Nirtana Teri Thompson, who has led the dances for twelve years, arranged candles around the fire, and we meditated for a few moments before the dances began. Then, in a spirit of reverence, we stood as Teri taught us the words and movements of the dances.

"Let my heart reflect thy light, Lord," we sang, as we faced the center of the circle, hands crossed on our hearts, then opening up and out as a symbolic gesture of receptivity.

"As the moon reflects the light of the sun." We turned to the person next to us, palm to palm . . .

"In love, always in love." Taking someone's hand, we made a half turn, then returned to face the center of the circle, our hands again over our hearts.

"Hu Allah, Allah hu Allah, Allah hu Allah, Allah hu," we sang, circling to the right and then to the left, symbolically releasing God's love in every direction.

As we moved, Teri continually reminded us that it didn't matter if we "messed up" the dance; it was about the worship in our hearts and the spiritual energy we created by being together. "We're dancing our prayers," she said. "If you're uncomfortable about using the name 'Allah,' remember that Arabic speakers all over the world, including Arabic-speaking Christians, call God 'Allah.' It's just another language."

Half of the people present, Teri told me later, had never done the dances, but everyone danced as if they'd been doing them all of their lives—not because our movements were perfect, but because we entered fully into the spirit of the dance. Closing our eyes, we concentrated on the Divine Presence among us, bumping into one another, apologizing the first few times, then taking the collisions in stride, and moving deeper into prayer and worship. As we danced, Teri sat in the middle of the circle, near the fire, and pounded an easy, quiet rhythm on her drums.

My introduction to these dances come through Shahabuddin at the Caravan of the Beautiful, and each time I've participated since then, I've felt more deeply the powerful sense of spirituality created through the message of the dances. As we join hands, I feel the bonds of community. When we turn in place, singing a Name of God, I sense God's love and purity deep within me. And as we move to face a partner, looking into that person's eyes (both Nirtana and Shahabuddin tell us to look gently and not to bore into the other person), I'm aware of the connection each of us shares—an essence created in the image of God.

In *Spiritual Dance and Walk*, Samuel Lewis gives eleven keys to help us embrace the spirit of the dance and make it a prayer of the heart: "Concentrate on the feeling deep within your heart," he writes, "and ignore the intellectual badgering that reprimands you for doing something 'wrong.' Concentrate on the sacred phrase given you by the dance leader and let it touch your being in a deeper and deeper way. Move together, concentrating on the unity that the dances evoke. And soar with your whole being, submitting yourselves to Allah/God 'in whom we live and move and have our being.'"

There's also a reminder for the musicians who set the tempo of the dance: "The music should accentuate the natural rhythm of the sacred phrase," he wrote, "and drummers should take particular note, allowing the sacred phrase to dominate. If you play your instrument correctly," wrote Lewis, "no one will even notice you. Isn't that wonderful?"

As with all Sufis, Lewis wanted the focus to be upon God, and used the admonition to remind us of one of Sufism's most valued attributes—humility.

While the sacred phrase is the most important element in the Dances of Universal Peace, the various movements of the body have symbolic meaning. When hands are joined or stretched towards the center of the circle, both of these movements represent unity. Hands placed upon our hearts reflect the spiritual journey within. Hands uplifted recognize the presence of God all around us. Moving together around the circle or spinning in place reminds us that we are microcosms of the always-moving universe.

Movements also create an actual, physical change. Certain movements, said Lewis, promote the "translucent Angelic moods hidden within us." As we move around the circle and gaze into the eyes of others, we evoke a sense of unconditional love, seeing in another the essence of the Divine. And as we chant in various sacred languages and mimic the movements from many religious traditions, we gain an immediate, accessible feeling for another tradition."

To understand the importance of movement, we only need to look at how it affects us in everyday life. When we rush some-where mindlessly, we're filled with tension and worry. When we walk slowly and look around us, a feeling of tranquility absorbs us, and we begin to appreciate the moment we're in. The rhythmic flow of Tai Chi, for instance, or the breath-conscious poses of yoga create an inner quietness, whereas a gesture such as shaking your fist at a driver who has just cut you off creates aggression and hostility.

These sacred movements don't bring God into our presence. God is always present. But creating an atmosphere in a room and in our hearts through symbolic and meaningful movements of our bodies helps bring God into our *awareness*. We close our eyes and search for God within. We dance with another, looking into their eyes, and we see God in another human being. Lifting our hands toward the heavens, then bringing them back to our hearts, we sense God's spirit within and without. As we turn in place, we feel the eternal movement of God through the mysterious yet perfect movement of the universe. It is the dance of *zikr*, and through it, we are remembering God.

....

Although most Sufi orders incorporate some sort of movement into their *zikrs,* each order varies in its approach and philosophy. Some movements begin slowly and symbolically and, as they proceed, increase in speed. Robert Gass, in his exhaustive research into the ritual of chant within numerous religious traditions, quotes Shaykh Robert Ragip Frager in explaining the reasons and results for this increasingly fast tempo:

"There is a powerful sense of energy, of joy arising in the heart and in the body," he says. "You are inexorably pulled into a different state of consciousness, close to God." At the end of this, writes Gass, there is an "exquisite" inner and outer silence.

I've found this to be true when watching others engaged in the *sema,* one of the most famous "dances" of Sufism, the whirling movement born of the divine friendship of Rumi and Shams. Every aspect of the *sema* is symbolic. The dervishes, explain Bayat and Jamnia, slowly walk around the room three times, each time kissing their teacher's hand. Then, suddenly, they throw off their black gowns, which symbolize their earthly bodies, and emerge in their "white gowns of eternal light, spinning around their axes as well as whirling around the center, as though the atoms were dancing around the sun."

The *sema,* however, is more than symbolic. Our bodies carry "within their very structure and cellular memory the circular motion of the stars, planets, and galaxies," writes Pir Vilayat Inayat Khan. These forces, he says, "are aroused when the body rotates." The *sema,* then, through its particular type of movement, brings about the divine energy of God present in the workings of the universe.

A form of the *sema* is used by other orders, who simply call it *whirling* or the *turn.* The most moving example of this I've ever seen came from a young dervish from California named Aziz, whom I saw whirl during *zikrs* in North Carolina and at various places in Turkey. Clearly, Aziz, as he whirls, utterly loses himself in God, and he does so regardless of whether he's whirling in an auditorium or in a quiet, holy spot among friends.

How imprinted upon my heart and mind is an evening in Istanbul, in a massive, sprawling *dergah* called *Ummi Sinan*, where about one hundred and thirty of us gathered in a massive room for *zikr*. As we repeated the Divine Names of God, Aziz suddenly moved into the large, open space in the center of the room. After bowing symbolically toward the place where a Master would traditionally stand, he removed his coat and began to slowly spin, his body turning in perfect rhythm as he moved around the circle— an image of the earth turning on its axis while it rotates around the sun.

After several rotations, a second man, Faruk, from Izmir, Turkey, entered the circle, bowed, removed his black coat, and accompanied Aziz. Then a third, Raqib, joined them. Their white robes cascaded around their bodies as they extended one hand toward heaven and the other toward earth.

As I sat absorbed, a lovely passage from Hazrat Inayat Khan's *The Music of Life* came to mind, which I later looked up and re-read. In the passage, Khan tells of the extraordinary effects of a snake charmer's music upon cobras in India:

> First they [the cobras] come out of the hole in which they live, and then there is a certain effect on their nervous system that draws them closer and closer to the sound of the *pungi*. They forget that instinct that is seen in every creature of protecting itself from the attack of man or of other creatures. At that time they absolutely forget; they do not see anyone or anything. They are then aroused to ecstasy . . . and as long as

this instrument is played the cobra continues to move in ecstasy. This shows us that, as well as the psychical effect and the spiritual effect that sound has on man, there is also a physical effect.

Aziz, Faruk, and Raqib moved to the sound within—the rhythmic voice of God. They were attuned to the divine music in their hearts and the soulful repetition of the names of God being voiced all around them. In ecstasy, a state of being in which only the Presence of God remains, the men whirled in the spirit of Rumi.

Perhaps fifteen minutes passed, perhaps thirty, but finally, the three men dropped to the floor, reluctant to leave their state of deep communion with God. The atmosphere of exquisite inner and outer silence engulfed the room.

CHAPTER SEVEN

Climbing the Mystic's Ladder

I will never forget my awakening.

For most of my life I had lived with very little spiritual imagination. I did everything in my power to live within the rigid and often strange set of rules I'd developed for myself. I believed there was no truth in any religion outside of my own, and I read the Bible, for the most part, looking for additional rules that would make me good.

One evening I found myself sitting in church on a Wednesday night listening to a man who is now my pastor, Dr. George Mason. That night, George was talking in his usual freestyle manner about heaven. He had been wrestling, he said, with the seemingly contradictory ideas found in Scripture about *purgatory*, of what many saw as the distinctive places called *heaven* and *paradise*, and how these ideas fit with the apostle Paul's statement that when we're "away from the body," we're "home with the Lord."

George then wrote the word *heaven* on the chalkboard, drew a line underneath, wrote the word *purgatory* under the line, then erased the line. What if, he mused, heaven and purgatory and paradise are simply different levels of the same place? What if, when we die, we enter into God's presence, but we don't enter into it fully? Though there's no time in eternity, maybe our souls will enter a realm, or a state, in which we become more and more aware of our impurities and attachments and, for the first time, we're able to more deeply grieve and surrender to God. We're in God's presence already, but as we open our hearts more fully to God's grace and glory, we begin to move into the "heavenly" state in which our hearts can experience it more and more fully.

I had never been in a church where the Bible was seen imaginatively and playfully. My own theological world came in black and white, not shades of gray. I rarely asked questions, because I thought I had all the answers. Suddenly, though, in the space of only a few minutes, a new way of thinking, and thus a new world, was opened to me. God, life, religion, spirituality, and Scripture all lost their starkness and their clear-cut interpretation. From that moment on, a new level of consciousness opened up for me. Vast worlds of many realms and levels lay spread before me, ready for me to begin feasting upon.

Awakening is not, as I used to think, a high level of spiritual achievement. Awakening is merely the realization that what you've held onto all your life without question isn't the only reality. For me, that didn't involve rejecting everything I believed; rather, it brought new imagination to everything. It allowed me to see beyond the surface, to penetrate more deeply into the *essence* of a teaching or law or story.

Mystical Judaism, for instance, interprets the Bible on four levels which correspond to four mystical worlds: *asiyah, yetzirah, beriyah,* and *atzilut. Asiyah* is a basic level of simple, literal inter-pretation. In *atzilut,* on the other hand, lies the world of profound mystery where you find the deepest meaning in the stories and teachings of Scripture. I had spent my life stuck in the world of *asiyah*. George's lesson that evening began to move me beyond it.

While that message became my awakening, I soon realized—joyfully—that I had merely put a toe on the path. I stood only at the trailhead. A beautiful, mysterious, unknown path lay before me and, at that moment, I knew I was ready to plunge into a spiritual adventure.

....

Mystics think of spirituality in terms of levels of attainment, marked by various characteristics and, less importantly, mystical experiences. For the person struggling along the path, being aware of where you are on the mystical path allows you to see down the road and instills a sense of how far you have to go.

Regardless of your level you should avoid feeling a sense of spiritual pride. Teachers and masters of the mystical path go to great lengths to warn us of the dangers inherent in focusing on what stage we're in as we travel the mystical path, reminding us that pride in our spiritual progress is the worst of all sins.

When someone imagines himself to have any kind of perfection, whether in knowledge or behavior, says Shaykh al-Shabrawi, he or she should spend some time reflecting on those who "died as disbelievers," having once thought themselves to be lovers of God."

The great Christian mystics echo these thoughts. The person who is proud of his spiritual progress, writes St. Maximos, is the one "who has not yet attained divine knowledge energized by love." St. Teresa of Avila wrote that perhaps God gave her mystical experiences "because she was so wretched." Good people don't need them, she states humbly. And Pseudo-Macarius, a Syrian monk of the fourth century, tells us that "[p]ride in making spiritual progress must be checked through . . . vigilance of the thoughts."

For those who have spiritual guides (and virtually all of the mystical traditions stress the importance of this), identifying a level of spirituality helps the teacher offer suggestions for spiritual practices and disciplines.

When modern-day author Paul Mariani spent thirty days in a guided spiritual retreat at a Jesuit monastery, one of the responsibilities included meeting daily with a spiritual director who gave him passages from the Bible and from St. Ignatius's *Spiritual Exercises*, chosen on the basis of what the guide felt he needed for his spiritual journey. Tibetan Buddhist masters also assign "practices tailored to [a person's] level of spiritual understanding."

Spiritual exercises can be difficult for me at times, not because I'm not self-disciplined, but because I tend to be overly so. I've never had a problem setting aside time to meditate and pray; my problem is that this time can become routine and rigid, making me forget the reason I'm praying and the focus of that prayer—God. While my Sufi teacher, Sherif Baba, offers solid, spiritual teaching, he believes equally in teaching his *mureeds* (or students) to attune to their own hearts, trusting the voice of God found there.

For me, dreams have been a strong source of guidance as I've begun learning about and traveling the mystical path. In one powerful dream, I climbed a mountain but came to a place that looked too vertical and difficult to climb. Though footholds marked the entire ascent, I was afraid I'd fall backwards and hurt myself. Finally encouraged by a few other people who had made the ascent, I began climbing.

At the top, I was surprised and delighted by several discoveries. First of all, the climb was relatively short, even if it was scary and a bit dangerous. Second, the mountain was *much* bigger than it looked at the bottom, with many more climbs ahead of me; had I seen that far up, I probably wouldn't have begun the journey. Third, the place where I stopped to rest was breathtakingly gorgeous.

When I woke from this dream, the symbolism was immediately apparent. Spiritual journeys are made in short spurts—one day at a time—one foot in front of the next. If we remain aware, whatever state we're in at the moment is filled with its own particular beauty, glory, and excitement. Yet we can't rest there forever. The path looms onward and upward, beckoning us to increasingly magnificent vistas.

·······

One of the things that makes the mystical journey unique for the spiritual traveler is the quest for ecstatic union with God, achieved as we progress through different "worlds," levels of reality, or heightened states of consciousness. To understand this better, we need to look briefly at the philosophy of *emanation,* which, in some mystical traditions, is the story of how we got here. Emanation is, to me, the single most fascinating aspect of mysticism.

Emanation is a philosophy of creation in which, in the beginning, God (or the "One," for the Neoplatonic mystics) "birthed" a level of creation just slightly lower than God. The particulars of the levels of creation vary within traditions, and even between mystics within a particular tradition, but generally, emanation is a process in which different realms (mind, soul, spiritual beings) flowed directly from the Being of God, with the final emanation resulting in the world in which we live, along with humankind.

The absolute importance of this for the mystic is that knowledge of these realms guides us on the path of return to God—a journey in which we travel spiritually through the various realms or worlds or levels of consciousness in our quest to re-unite with God.

Some time ago I was talking about this with a Christian friend who said he was uncomfortable with the concept of emanation. "It takes the will of God out of creation," he said.

"Yes," I said. "That's what's so lovely about it! It brings creation fully into the realm of Love. God is so full of love that God burst forth, so to speak, giving birth to creation. Creation wasn't a dry, willful decision. It was an action that stemmed from what we call *the heart*."

"The very nature of pure love—of God," I went on, "is to create. Just like it's the nature of God to be good and to love—and God can be and do nothing else—so it's the nature of God to birth. This isn't limiting God; it's understanding that God is able to exist only according to God's own nature. So with emanation. It isn't limiting God to say that God 'had' to create. Creation is merely the essence of Love and of God. God could no more withhold creation than God could commit an act of evil."

The important aspect of emanation is that as we ponder these "worlds" emanating from God, we learn the path of ascent—or return. Mystics teach that, yes, you can experience God through the realm of nature and the beauty in this world. You can understand certain truths about God and about spirituality through the intellect. But in order to directly and fully re-unite with God in a mystical sense, you have to rise above these lower worlds and experience God in the realm where the distinctions of time and space disappear.

For the Sufi, ascent to God comes about by repetition—with the tongue and with sincerity of heart—of God's Divine Names, and through absorbing spiritual teaching until it becomes a part of your own soul. A spiritual guide or teacher is essential but she isn't an intellectual teacher. Rather, she helps you discover where you are on the path, and aids you in finding the disciplines which will help you purify and be in touch with the guidance of your own heart.

There is no single "right" way to make this mystical ascent to God. St. John of the Cross compares the ascent to climbing "a ladder of love," beginning with a longing, swooning, and "languishing" of the soul, and ending with the souls becoming "wholly assimilated to God," with all mysteries and secrets being revealed.

Like Sufism, some aspects of Jewish mysticism focus on a Divine Name of God as they begin the ascent. For the Jewish mystic, the Most Holy Name is YHVH which, unlike the Names in Sufism, can't be pronounced. Instead, the Jewish mystic meditates silently on the Divine Name until mystical ascension occurs. Sikhs also commune and draw closer to God through repetition of God's names in Sanskrit, Persian, and Arabic, as do Hindus—a practice they refer to as *namajapa*. The Hesychasts of the Eastern Christian tradition recite the "Jesus Prayer," focusing on the name of Jesus.

One of my favorite Christian mystics, Pseudo-Dionysius, had an interesting twist on reciting the Divine Names. For him, the person seeking union with God should first meditate on each attribute (or Name) of God, beginning with those that most closely represent God—abstract ones such as light or goodness, for instance. As one meditates, he or she works through numerous attributes of God until she reaches those that are furthest from God's reality—concrete forms such as friend, say, or the human emotion of anger.

To reach a state or level in which the soul experiences ecstatic union with God, though, the seeker then has to meditate on what God is *not*. God "is not power, nor is [God] light. . . . nor is [God] eternity or time," Dionysius says. "God cannot be grasped by the understanding, since God is neither knowledge nor truth. God is not kingship. God is not wisdom. God is neither one nor oneness, divinity nor goodness." And so on.

For Dionysius, the person seeking union with God must enter
a state in which the soul can no longer form intellectual concepts
about God, but can only stand in awe, enraptured by the uniqueness
of God's being and beauty, unable to apprehend God with any
degree of genuine accuracy or intellectual certainty.

Isaac of Nineveh, one of the best-known Syriac Fathers of the
church, quoted the "holy Dionysios" to remind us that we use
metaphors to describe God only when our souls need something
"to hold onto." But when our soul is elevated in spiritual ecstasy
and union, the intellect "forgets itself and everything else here." It
becomes swallowed up in the Spirit, "dwell[ing] in wonder in that
delightful glory."

What, then, is this ecstatic union that the mystics seek? For
the Sufi, it's *fana*, a state in which we lose our egos and only a
blissful awareness of God remains. The idea of *fana*—the "passing
away of the personal self"—was the aspect of Sufism that most
deeply attracted Thomas Merton. This was also a major theme of
the Syriac Church Fathers. Joseph the Visionary, among others,
wrote of *msarrquta*, or self-emptying, that accompanies the "exalted
stages" of the spiritual path.

Union, however, is perhaps one of the most misunderstood
aspects of mysticism. Ecstatic union with God isn't, for instance,
a literal detachment from earthly life. In fact, it can be seen as the
complete opposite, for union with God brings the deepest sense of
compassion and concern for everything that happens here, for
every creature and aspect of creation. The mystic who is no longer
absorbed in his or her own affairs becomes utterly absorbed in
caring for others. This person no longer sees Jew or Gentile, Arab
or Caucasian, male or female, white or black. He or she cares
about all human beings, all of nature, and all of what is being done
in the name of progress to our fragile, lovely earth.

Not long ago my Sunday school class spent a few weeks watching and discussing a video of Benedictine oblate Joan D. Chittister in which she gives a talk about Benedictine spirituality. Though I was mesmerized by every word, one part of her lecture rings repeatedly in my heart.

Chittister tells of a recent interview in which a reporter asked a high-ranking official of the American military why no estimates of the number of Iraqi dead were reported from the recent war. The answer, Chittister says, was this: "That is a number in which I have no interest whatsoever." Chittister demands that we break the "secular silence," and ask the question: "*Why don't you?*"

The mystical seeker who has experienced union with God—*even if for a single moment*—does ask this question. The mystical seeker who has experienced union with God is forever changed, cares less for herself, desires a deeper purity, loves others, respects nature, and cares more for our earth. We leave *fana*, writes the Sufi master Yaşar Nuri Özturk, but we return to the earth "radically transformed."

Sherif Baba reminds us that like Rumi, we must "dance" the holy teachings. "Rumi put his left foot down on one spot and with his right foot he went all around," Baba says. "He opened his right hand to the air and opened his left hand to the earth. But what does this mean? Was he giving a show? No, he was taking from Allah [with his right hand] and giving to the people [with his left hand]."

Hazrat Inayat Khan tells the story of the Sufi master Bullah Shah. As a child, his teacher taught him the first letter of the Arabic alphabet: *alif*. While the other children in the class progressed to master the entire alphabet, Shah remained on this one letter. Weeks passed and the teacher, frustrated with the boy, sent him home to his parents. His parents hired private tutors, but months later, they gave up in disappointment. Shah would not progress past *alif*.

Not wanting to be a burden on anyone, Shah ran away to the forest where, as Khan tells it, he saw the "manifestation of alif . . . as the grass, the leaf, the tree, branch, fruit, and flower." The same alif, Khan writes, became the mountain and hill, the stones and rocks, every animal, in himself and in others.

Finally, after he had mastered this lesson, he returned to his teacher, who had long ago forgotten him. But Bullah Shah had not forgotten the teacher who had taught him his most important lesson—one that he had spent his entire life absorbing. Bowing before his old teacher, Bullah said, "I have prepared the lesson you so kindly taught me; will you teach me anything more?"

What if we took a single lesson and thoroughly absorbed it? Rather than being gluttons for more knowledge, what levels of spirituality might we reach if we remained with one holy sentence— a single, spiritually potent concept? The Hebrew writers asked us to love God with our entire being and to love others as we love ourselves, and Jesus said that such love summed up the entire law and prophets. Perhaps we should spend an entire lifetime mastering this single command—that of *ashk*, or divine love.

Traveling the mystical path isn't about learning more or doing more. It's about *absorbing* what we *already* know—a vastly more difficult task. The Sufis tell us that a Divine Name uttered one time with the utmost sincerity, from the deepest reaches of our heart, can plunge us into realms that some, seeking half-heartedly for a lifetime, never reach. When everything disappears except for a pure longing for God—even for a moment—we're on the mystical path. My own desire is to capture more of those moments.

CHAPTER EIGHT

Finding a Spiritual Guide

I'm sitting on a bus, leaving Cappadocia, and looking out onto an otherworldly landscape. Some have described these conelike mountainous protrusions as moonlike. Using natural openings within these rocks, people began two thousand years ago to build homes, churches, and even monasteries inside these rocks, and many continue to live in these beautiful cave-homes today.

It's January and typically very cold and snowy this time of year, but the air is merely chilly and as the sun blazes through the windows, I, cold-natured person that I am, move into a position where I can feel the full force of its heat.

Baba, who's sitting in the front seat, looks around the bus happily and spots me sitting by myself, so he gets up and moves down the aisle, the bus jostling him from side to side. Though Baba uses a translator when he's teaching in order to communicate better, he knows enough English to carry on brief conversations. "Usually very cold in Cappadocia in January," Baba says, as he slides into the seat next to me. "But I told Allah, 'Allah! The Americans are coming to Turkey!' And Allah made it beautiful for you."

Baba asks me if I'm having a good time. We chat for a few minutes, then he returns to his seat, waving out the window. "Bye bye, Cappadocia!" he says, cheerfully.

As Baba returns to his seat, I'm reminded of the many reasons I'm drawn to him. He finds delight in everything—in God, other people, the beautiful land surrounding us, and even in a good meal. Though he encourages us to become increasingly pure, we feel accepted and loved when we fail. Serious about spirituality and the mystical path, he loves a good joke and his sense of humor enlivens his lessons. Because of these things, I'm inspired to try to imitate him in his joyful and wholehearted devotion to God.

Spiritual guides are not traditionally part of our culture in the West, especially in evangelical churches. My own tradition emphasizes the "priesthood of the believer," which I love, but which can, if we're not careful, lead us to discard the advice and example of others.

Many religions, however, including Christianity, Buddhism, Sufism, and Hinduism, traditionally value the role of the personal, spiritual teacher. "To be guided by a mature and advanced spiritual soul-friend is absolutely necessary for the Christian," writes Fr. George A. Maloney, author, priest, and founder and director of the John XXIII Institute for Eastern Christian Studies at Fordham University. "Beginners should search for a person . . . who knows from personal experience of the 'heart' the path to perfection."

A Hindu follows the guru with whom he feels a close, heart-felt affinity. In traditional Buddhism, the guidance of a master is indispensable. Modern American Buddhists often practice on their own, but Eastern Buddhists remind us that when we meditate through the direction of a personal guide, we can more easily avoid blind spots.

Likewise, Sufis emphasize the importance of choosing a spiritual guide. This person is someone who has wholeheartedly devoted herself to a particular path, has attained a high degree of purity, and enjoys continual communion with God. A spiritual guide is someone with whom we resonate in the deepest part of our beings, a person who seems "God-sent" to us, and one whom we can trust and respect.

What, then, about our pastors, rabbis, and other leaders? Aren't they spiritual guides and teachers? Of course. My own pastor continually opens new doors of spirituality for me. He was my spiritual "awakener," and continues to give me fresh visions of God and spirituality. George is an inspiration and example to me of humility, kindness, and joy in serving God. His involvement with the local schools, in interfaith work, and his generosity in giving to organizations that help others in need, spurs me to do the same.

Why, then, do I have another spiritual guide?

Because I want to travel the mystical path. I want to experience the unveiling of the mysteries hidden on each level, and tune into the subtle voices that continually whisper to me and direct my life. My pastor would be the first to tell me that he isn't a mystic and thus wouldn't be an adequate guide for this path.

I do, however, find my various avenues of spirituality complementary. Each enriches my spiritual life in a unique way. For instance, I go to my church to celebrate the teachings and love of Jesus. Christianity was the family into which I was born. Like my blood family, they're the people with whom I grew up and with whom I share special lifelong bonds. I love old hymns and pews and organs and the spiritual connection I feel with God and other people in church. I also love my weekly visits to those in my church who are homebound.

I also regularly attend prayer services at synagogue—usually Temple Emanu-El in Dallas. Indeed, I doubt I'll ever love another religion like I do Judaism. While the church feels like family, Judaism feels like the love I found as an adult. All of the rituals of the prayer service move me—the prayers themselves, the melodic chanting, the kissing of the Torah as the rabbis bring it down the aisles, the *kiddush* to end the service—every aspect fills me with a sense of God's presence.

Along with these loves I've found another: Sufism. My Sufi teacher guides me more deeply into the *mysteries* of the spiritual world. I'm learning to tune into the deepest recesses of my heart and to find the place where I meet the Divine. I'm discovering the common bonds I share with all other humans. I'm increasingly aware of the pulsating life in constant motion all around me. The lessons I've learned throughout my life have, through Sufism, penetrated my heart more deeply.

....

Because Sufi teachers emphasize personal, inner guidance, they aren't concerned with group uniformity. They value us as unique individuals who learn and grow in different ways. A Sufi teacher's goal is to help the *mureed*, or student, gradually attain a quiet and pure heart—one that is constantly attuned to the voice of God within and without.

In Sufism, teachers are said to be attuned to the spiritual levels and needs of their *mureeds*, and typically, they suggest particular meditations appropriate for the individual.

Sufism also emphasizes what, in some orders, is called *sohbet*, or spiritual discourse. Again, this isn't a sermon like you'd hear in a church or synagogue. Rather, *sohbet* is a spontaneous, verbal reflection: stories and parables intended to awaken the listener to new states of spiritual consciousness. Music and prayer and feedback through questions or comments are also often part of *sohbet*, making it a time of group participation.

In Sufism, the connection of the teacher with the *mureed* is mystical in nature. The well-known Sufi author Llewellyn Vaughan-Lee writes that the most important teaching that the Sufi master passes on isn't verbal, but a "direct communion *from heart to heart*." If you've ever felt "attuned" to someone—an intimate friend, a spouse, a parent or sister—you'll understand what this means. Husbands and wives are sometimes said to look physically alike after being together for many years. Our facial features, gestures, and emotional makeup begin to reflect that of our spouse.

An unconscious taking on of someone's characteristics to whom we're close is common, and mimics the relationship of a *mureed* to his spiritual guide. Gradually, mysteriously, we find ourselves emanating the same beauty—the love and joy and kindness—that pours from our teacher.

Recently I sat under the teaching of the Venerable Khenpo Tsewang Gyatso Rinpoche, a respected Tibetan Buddhist teacher. In one of the handouts I received, the mystical relationship of the teacher to the student was highlighted in this way: "[E]nlightened knowledge can be transmitted from one person to another, as a flame can pass from one candle to the next, illuminating each according to his potential."

Enlightened knowledge is simply an "aha" moment in which you go beyond hearing a lesson and even beyond understanding it. It's a moment when the *essence* of the lesson comes alive in your heart and life.

The Sufi teacher's presence can be mystical in other ways, too. I've discovered this in delightful and amazing ways. Over the past twenty years, I've made numerous spiritual retreats, often alone, but at other times with a spiritual community. In the past, when I returned home from these retreats, I needed several days to readjust. I'd been on a spiritual high, absorbed in God twenty-four-seven, and then, when I returned home, I was thrown back into a myriad of responsibilities. My workload seemed to crush out the pure, elevated state my soul had been basking in, and I felt a mild depression, irritability, and withdrawal from other people. Though these negative feelings never lasted more than a few days, they were always frustrating.

Not long ago I realized that this need for readjustment had changed within me. This had begun with a strange experience that happened during my return from Turkey. As I was about to board the plane with Baba, Jem, and a few other Turkish friends waving from the gate, I felt a crushing sadness. As I sat on the plane, weeping as I always do when I'm leaving a spiritual retreat, I suddenly swung around and looked behind me. A Turkish woman whom I didn't know glanced up, smiled, and went back to reading her book. I could have sworn that as I had turned my head I had seen Baba sweep past me and move into the seat behind me. Chills crept up my spine.

A few minutes later, before we had begun taxiing down the runway, it happened again, only this time I thought I saw him slide into a seat across from me. Again, a strange feeling engulfed me. Just as suddenly, the pall lifted, and I felt I wasn't leaving Baba behind at all. In fact, months before that, when I had asked how he could be my teacher living at nearly the opposite end of the country from me, he had simply said that "we aren't apart." Was this in some way actually true? Was Baba's spirit—in whatever way we might feel comfortable envisioning this—with me?

The days that followed my departure from Turkey seemed to confirm this. There was absolutely no period of readjustment, no crankiness when I returned home, and no devastating sense of loss. Instead, I simply retained the elevated spiritual feelings for a while, then gradually, eased into a mood of serenity and quiet joy. Something within me had been permanently changed. I felt closer to God, and a little more aware of God's continual presence. I reacted less often and less severely to upsetting situations. An old, deep pain and lack of forgiveness suddenly clawed its way to the surface, exposed itself, and then—softly, incrementally—began to dissolve.

Since that trip to Turkey, I've taken several spiritual retreats and have felt no need for readjustment when I returned home. Instead, I bring back a little bit of a new me. I feel a sense of euphoria which, though it doesn't last in intensity, lasts in its effects. It's as if I haven't left the spiritual retreat altogether, as if I've brought a tiny piece of it back with me. That continual sense of God's presence is precisely what a Sufi master wants to instill.

A few months ago I called my friend Shekibe to chat. Shekibe and I had been roommates in Turkey and had formed a bond. When she answered her phone she began whispering and I realized that I'd called during *sohbet*. Usually she didn't have her cell-phone on during *sohbet*, she told me, but she'd been expecting an important call.

After talking for a few minutes, Shekibe suddenly told me, with excitement in her voice, that she was going to put her cell-phone beside Baba so I could listen in. Shuffling sounds followed and I pictured Shekibe tiptoeing to the front of the room, crawling through the cushions, and placing her cell-phone on the floor between Baba and Jem.

For several minutes I sat in my car, unable to hear a thing, then Shekibe's voice returned, whispering, "Can you hear Baba? No? Hold on then." More shuffling sounds followed as Shekibe

figured out a way to prop the phone up a little higher, and I then
heard Baba's and Jem's voices. Though I still couldn't make out
what they were saying, I remained on the phone for nearly ten
minutes, soaking in the atmosphere, grateful to be "connected" to
my Sufi teacher and friends, even if that meant only hearing the
sounds of their voices.

·········

For the Sufi, the spiritual guide, or *murshid*, leads us to find
God within our own hearts. In one of the most significant dreams
I've ever had, I dreamt I was looking for a jewelry store and asked
several people for directions. One tried to give me directions but
because they didn't know where I was coming from, they failed to
get me even to the first street. Another began to give me directions
in a confident manner, then began faltering and ended up telling
me they didn't know how to get me to the jewelry store. A third
person just shrugged.

Then I found myself next to a Sufi friend who led me to a
vantage point in which I could look out on an endless expanse of
mountains. Everywhere I looked I saw the most magnificent beauty.
Then my friend simply pointed in a general direction toward one
of the peaks.

In my dream, I felt confused. What kind of directions are
these, I wondered? How am I to find the jewelry store—this place
of tremendous value and beauty—by having someone point a finger
in a vague direction?

When I woke the message was immediate and clear. The
way to the kingdom of God—a state of intimacy and the closest
communion—isn't set out step by step. I'll have valleys to walk
through, which St. John of the Cross called the "dark night of the
soul." I'll have some steep climbs ahead of me and will sometimes
feel lost and tired and hopeless as I walk towards paradise. Yet I'll

always be surrounded by unimaginable beauty. And if I keep my heart and mind and spiritual eyes set on the lovely place I'm walking through at any given moment, I'll never be overwhelmed by the mountains I have yet to climb.

Sherif Baba asks the question:

"How did Moses go up to Mt. Sinai and speak to God? How did he get the Ten Commandments from up there? I go to mountains. I don't find anything there. I get good oxygen. Nice air. Beauty. But people think, 'I'll go to Mount Sinai [because God is there]. I'll go to the Mount of Olives [because God is there].'

"But God doesn't live in these mountains. People have to search within themselves. They have to walk through [their own] mountains and swim across [their own] rivers and in [their own] oceans. All of that is inside this tiny being here. Hazrat Ali had this saying: 'the human being is a small creature yet a huge [great] creation.'"

Baba is saying that my dream of the vast and gorgeous mountain range lies within me. God's majesty will become ever more apparent and vivid as I travel deeper and further. It's an adventurous journey, because I don't have precise instructions for the sojourn. I'll simply have to greet each day with the faith that I can take the next step, and as I go, to try to remember God with each breath I take. Knowing that God is with me during the valleys and the steep climbs, and wherever I am, I can inhale the eternal beauty of God's presence.

I like those directions.

CHAPTER NINE

Creating an Altar

*T*his morning I sat, as I always do, before a beautiful altar, though its beauty isn't in its elaborate decor. It doesn't have any sculptures meticulously carved by famous or even talented artists. Although it has caught the eye of visitors in my home, it doesn't inspire the kind of breath-catching awe that, say, the altar in a large church inspires. Two things, though, make the altar in my home beautiful. One is the care I've given to its creation. A couple of years ago I began searching for an object that I could use to set up as an altar. I wanted something unusual—an altar that exuded a mysterious spirituality, a piece of art that I connected with and that would call me to daily prayer.

After looking for months Mike and I ran across a gorgeous antique-looking chest at an imports store. Etched on the chest's cover were masses of what looked to be chalices, urns, and incense burners of various shapes and sizes surrounded by a border of leaves and spirals. We bought it and once home, Mike removed the cover and legs—which curl in lovely shapes in different directions—from the chest and attached the legs to the cover, creating a stunning altar at precisely the needed height.

During the following year, I gradually filled the altar (and the area surrounding it) with items that I considered holy and which held special meaning for me. A small statue of St. Francis which sits beside the altar holds prayer beads and rosaries blessed by Catholic priests, Sufi saints, and monks from Tibetan Buddhism. It also holds one of my most precious possessions—an acorn that Mike picked up for me as we walked along the paths of Assisi.

My Jewish prayer book and an engraved Hebrew necklace rest on a corner of my altar, along with a framed copy of the "Peace Prayer" of St. Francis in Italian, purchased at his mausoleum. Holy sand, blessed by Tibetan monks at the closing ceremony of the creation of a sand mandala, fills a tiny, jeweled box, and flowers which a friend gave me from a float used during one of the most holy days for Hindus still glow with color a year after they were plucked from the earth.

My Bible sits there, as well as a framed prayer of Hazrat Inayat Khan, some Sufi material that guides me in devotions, and a picture of my deceased, much-loved dad, with whom I've had spiritual communions that I could never explain on an intellectual level. A picture of Sherif Baba hangs on my wall, nearby.

But what has made this altar most beautiful is the sense of holiness that's created as I sit there each day. Some places are holy because of miracles that have occurred there, but others are holy because of the accumulation of prayers. The altar in my home, I believe, becomes increasingly sacred each day as I sit in front of it, releasing my thoughts, cares, worries—even the comparatively trivial joys of life—and entering into the sheer, ecstatic presence of God.

For as long as I can remember, I've had a daily "quiet time" with God. These moments draw me closer to God, and I often find strength through prayer and reading Scripture to tackle difficult periods in my life.

The devotion that I've enjoyed for the past year or so, however, has been entirely different from these past quiet times. I still verbalize prayers. I chant some of the Divine Names of God, and I sometimes reflect on a portion of the Bible or pray from my Jewish prayer book.

But the most important part of this time, the part that has made the most dramatic and lasting changes in my life and my relationship with God, is a time that was missing from my earlier devotional experiences. It consists of the moments when I sit quietly, both before and after my verbal prayers, soaking up the spiritual energy that permeates the room. My heart elevates in a way that makes me feel as if I'm being transported to another world.

Almost always, I'll end the time singing the "Peace Prayer" of St. Francis, put to music by the Franciscan monk and musician, John Michael Talbot:

> Lord, make me an instrument of your peace.
> Where there is hatred, let me sow love.
> Where there is injury, pardon.
> And where there is doubting, let me bring your faith.
> Lord, make me an instrument of your peace.
> Where there is despairing, let me bring hope.
> Where there is darkness, your light.
> And where there is sadness, let me bring your joy."
> O Divine Master, grant that I might seek
> Not so much to be consoled, as to console.
> To be understood, as to understand.
> And not so much to be loved, as to love another.

Most mornings, as I end *zikr*, my focused remembrance of God, I sing this song, slowly, with my eyes closed, letting each line penetrate my heart. Afterward, I sit for several minutes, not thinking about the words of the song, but simply breathing in the divine energy created by a deeply felt utterance of this prayer.

During the day, when I'm stressed, if someone verbally attacks me, or if things simply aren't going my way, I can close my eyes and, without verbally repeating this prayer, feel that same energy and, often, I'm lifted beyond the cares, hurts, or anger of the moment. While I don't walk around with a continual aura of peace and divinity (I'm far from a saint), I do find that I'm increasingly able to find this sense of holiness in the midst of potentially explosive situations.

Hazrat Inayat Khan reminds us that human beings affect the atmospheric vibrations all around us, creating an aura of tranquility or of tension that other people can sense. The space surrounding us takes on the same "rhythm" as our feelings or moods at any given time.

Khan also wrote that every single thought, action, and word remains in the atmosphere. "[W]hen something is thrown into space," he writes, "space does not lose it. . . . It has received it and it holds it."

Thinking about Khan's words has affected my life in powerful ways. For one thing, I'm more careful about angry words and emotions, about gossip and jealousy, about vindictive or harmful actions. I don't want to contribute to an atmosphere already tainted with ill intentions, violence, and hatred. Instead, I want to offer the loving emotions of kindness, compassion, joy, grace, and hope.

As I meditate on the heartfelt prayers of St. Francis, of the Hebrew saints, or of the Sufi shaykhs, I capture some little spark of their spirit which accumulates and changes the way I live and think and commune with God throughout the day. The apostle Paul reminds us of the Sufi's desire to rip away the veils of illusion so we can, day by day, bring healing to ourselves and others by becoming more like God, when he eloquently writes: "And all of us, with unveiled faces, seeing the glory of the Lord as though reflected in a mirror, are being transformed into the same image from one degree of glory to another."

....

I began serious meditation a few years ago and, like many people, I hated it. The aversion that beginners feel towards meditation often stems from the agonizing efforts of trying to sit still and quiet the noise that chatters incessantly in our heads. But the main problem for me wasn't my inability to sit still nor to quiet myself inwardly. I had done that to some degree for many years. Rather, I struggled with feelings that my meditation was more about myself than about God. Since one of my goals in meditation is to experience and know God in a deeper and more experiential way, it bothered me to think that meditation might be more about myself than it is about God.

What I soon discovered was that meditation *is indeed about me*! When I sit at the altar in my home and still my intellect and open my heart, praying in the deepest recesses of my soul, I'm not "conjuring up" God. God is *always* present. I'm not trying to pry God into action. God is *always* active. I'm not even attempting to persuade God to fill me with divine attributes. God is always ready to do this.

Rather, meditation acknowledges God's activity and presence and glory, and creates the space and conditions within that allow you to *manifest* this ever-present and always-active Presence. It's like walking down a busy city street, people bustling everywhere, horns honking, planes flying above your head, and then you detect the sound of a gregarious mockingbird somewhere nearby. The beautiful call is distinct but you have to stop, concentrate, and listen intensely in order to block out the other noises and tune into the peaceful, lilting song.

To some Christians, talking about "altered states of consciousness"—even mentioning those words—is frightening,
because it sounds like a drug-induced euphoria rather than an
experience of God. But our everyday, typical state of consciousness
centers around our work, families, goals, concerns, and worries,
and we do indeed have to alter our state of mind by sitting quietly,
or doing some kind of spiritual practice, until we begin to sense
ourselves moving into a deep, quiet state of being. When we do
this, a powerful sense of the presence of God arises, and we realize
that we've tuned into a deeper consciousness of God.

This is why people who meditate focus on the breath. Being
aware of the simple act of taking in air and releasing it stems the
flow of our noisy thinking and moves our attention inward. As
many of us know, the same word in Hebrew, *ruach*, is interpreted both
as *breath* and *spirit*. As we sit conscious of the intake and outflow of
our breath, we're able just to *be* with God. This breath, this spirit,
is our very flow of life. Rejuvenation and rebirth engulf us as we
inhale, and the earth receives and transforms the poisons that we
release in exhalation.

For many Sufis, breathing has symbolic meaning and purpose.
Rhythmic breathing and moving usually accompany the chanting
of the Divine Names of God, and in some orders, the teacher gives
instructions for the breathing and movements before the chanting
begins. In other orders, meditators may simply follow the patterns
of the shaykh.

Take one of the many symbols and breathing patterns for the
common Sufi chant of *La ilaha illa 'llah*. One suggestion for this
zikr, or meditation, is to chant *La ilaha* on the outbreath, imagining
that "murky water is being suctioned from a silted well" as all our
self-delusions, faults, negative attitudes, obsessions, and impurities
are breathed out, being absorbed by the earth (or discarded by God),

which (or who) cleanses and purifies. The inhalation, taken while chanting *illa 'llah*, is felt as the sun breath, or the "breath of love," and flows like a current, or like light, radiating through our bodies and deep into our hearts.

The similarity between the breathing patterns and symbolism of the hesychastic prayer of the Eastern Orthodox monks and the Sufis intrigued Thomas Merton. In one of his talks, Merton explained to his novices that a disciple sits before his teacher, breathing rhythmically with him, while chanting *La ilaha illa 'llah*. As the exhaling breath "turns everything out," the inhalation "breathes in love, desire, and total concentration on God."

Arabic, being a Semitic language, is very similar to Hebrew, and praying in languages with such lovely cadence and vibrant resonance can bring about deep and powerful feelings, maybe because we're connecting with something closer to the primal aspects of our mind—ancient languages considered holy and mysterious.

Sufis chant God's Names in Arabic, believing that the very sound invokes a particular attribute. The most holy name in Arabic—Allah—is pronounced with the emphasis on the second syllable, and the recitation of this name has the sound and feel of a sigh of longing. Al-LAHHHHH.

Chanting the Divine Names of God in a language that is considered holy and sacred may affect our subconscious in mysterious ways. In the late 1700s, a German physicist, Ernst Chladni, constructed a simple acoustic device called a *tonoscope* in which visual configurations represented various sounds such as "oh," "ah," and "oo."

As Chladni spoke different sounds into the mouthpiece of the tonoscope onto a layer of fine-grained sand, the granules moved into the shapes of mandalas, which varied according to the sounds Chladni made. The amazing thing is that this only worked with ancient, sacred languages such as Hebrew and Sanskrit. Nothing occurred when modern languages were intoned!

Is there really something to the sacredness of these ancient languages? Besides Hebrew, Arabic, and Sanskrit, the Catholic church has long considered Latin a sacred language, using it, until recently, during prayer services and for the Mass. Certainly God is always present and not more inclined to hear and answer prayers recited in these languages. But perhaps there is some kind of subtle and mysterious awakening of *our souls* that occurs when we pray in a holy language. Perhaps *we* become more present to God as we chant and pray in languages that have been considered holy for hundreds (or thousands) of years. Whatever the case may be, it's important to understand that all of us, regardless of our religion, are praying to one God. Those who pray to Allah, for instance, aren't praying to some kind of distinctive "Islamic" God. Allah is simply the Arabic word for God, and people, including Christians, who live in Arabic-speaking countries use the name *Allah* to refer to God.

La ilaha illa 'llah. "There is no God but God," chant the Sufis.

Shema Israel, Adonai Ehloheinu, Adonai Echod. "The Lord (YHVH) our God; the Lord (YHVH) is One," say the Jews.

"[I]s God the God of Jews only? Is he not the God of Gentiles also? Yes, of Gentiles also, since God is one." echoes the apostle Paul.

Muslims, Jews, and Christians avow that only one God exists. Modern Hindus also believe that the various "deities" are merely names and attributes of one divine Being. Many other religions that seem polytheistic often have one high, supreme God with lesser "gods" (in some cases, similar to our concept of angels) in God's service.

Each religion has different concepts of God, but then so do individual Christians among themselves, individual Jews among themselves, Muslims, Hindus and so on. In my own Sunday school class, discussions of God reveal all the different ways we, even in our comparatively tiny group, think about and experience God.

When I attend worship services at Christian denominations other than my own, I have an entirely different experience of God. The collective mind-set differs from that of my denomination and rather than sit back and observe as an outsider, I try to enter into the experience and to see and worship God as they do. My relationship with God has been deeply enriched by getting outside of my own spiritual skin and putting on the spiritual skins of others. Each religion, every denomination and individual can add to and deepen my experience of God.

· · · · · · · · · · · ·

Initially I was a suspicious and reluctant meditator, but now I cannot imagine a day without it. Typically, I pray and meditate and do *zikr* at my personal altar, but I also find a powerful, sacred power in holy places and in nature, and when I can, I spend time in prayer and meditation in these places as well.

Nature has always been a place where people feel a close sense of communion with God. I'm fortunate to live only about a mile from the largest wilderness area in the Dallas/Fort Worth metroplex, a reserve with peaceful trails and wildlife (including a cougar!). When I have extra time, I walk down the creek, spread out my jacket to sit on, close my eyes, and open myself to God's magnificent presence apparent in the beauty around me.

At other times, I sit in my backyard swing, engulfed by mimosas, sycamores, and fruitless mulberries, and listen to the sound of a creek running along the back boundary of my yard and to the birds who flutter about. Though I've begun learning to identify the birds by their calls and appearance, I don't need to know anything about them to have my soul uplifted by the divine hand that continuously breathes life and beauty into this world.

Two carolina wrens call exuberantly to each other across the creek. A flaming red cardinal casually snaps sunflower seeds from my bird feeder. I inhale the tangy smell of the trees and grass, the sweet fragrance of the roses and honeysuckle. These sights, sounds, and smells fill me with divine joy.

I'll never forget the pilgrimage Mike and I made to Assisi, walking high on the breathtakingly beautiful mountain where St. Francis walked, pausing to make tiny crosses from twigs, tying the pieces together with tufts of grass, and placing them on the natural altars created by other pilgrims. The sight of the Franciscan monks moving from one duty to the next in a quiet spirit of reverence created an atmosphere that pulsated with the Divine.

Many traditions also revere graves as places of holiness. Catholics traditionally flock to locations where miracles and visions have reportedly taken place, and tombs of saints are considered places of great holiness and power. Many Hasidic Jews regularly visit the graves of their *rebbes*, or spiritual leaders, and some have life-changing experiences there.

When I visited Turkey with Sherif Baba and members of his community, we spent much of our time reciting *zikr* at the tombs of dervishes and shaykhs. At the mosque where Shams, Rumi's teacher, is reportedly buried, I was utterly overwhelmed by a feeling I've experienced only a few times since then. My heart seemed to open with a raw vulnerability, and I had an agonizing awareness of my physical separation from the beauty and holiness surrounding me, accompanied by the thought that if I couldn't embrace it fully, I'd die. Three times I fled the mosque, uncertain of what was happening and insecure in my ability to cope with it. The third time I didn't return. The experience was too overwhelming.

Those moments, however, left with me a deeper peace and a lasting sense of the majesty and awesome holiness of God. Again, I think of the prophet Isaiah's vision of God, which was so powerful that he felt the very foundations of the temple tremble. The sounds of angels uttering ecstatic words of praise in the holy Presence of God echoed in his ears. When an angel touched his lips with a fiery coal, his soul was cleansed and purified, and made capable of a spectacular encounter with God.

Yet while few of us have these kinds of visions or mystical, direct experiences of God, we all come close to God as we learn to block out all desires and thoughts except God. We can learn to do this through meditation. Nature and other sacred places fill us with a sense of the Divine, but it's when our hearts are pure and utterly open that the glory of God fills us in the same wondrous way that God's glory filled the temple in Isaiah's vision. We are that temple, says the apostle Paul, and it is in us that God wants to reveal his majestic holiness.

Some time ago, Mike, who had begun meditating for the purpose of relieving stress, decided to use this time to pray, not with words, but by communing with his heart. In Mike's words, he "envisioned his soul reaching towards God," asking with his heart to know and experience God in a more intimate way.

As he lay on the floor, opening himself to God's Divine Presence, he felt a hand pressing upon his chest, near his heart. Startled, he opened his eyes, thinking I'd come into the room and had sat down beside him, so tangible was the presence. At the moment of the touch, however, Mike felt a sense of peace and love that he'd rarely, if ever, felt before. It was as if he'd been carrying around a heavy object, he later told me, that he'd become accustomed to, and someone had reached over and suddenly removed it. When he left his place of meditation, he carried with him a profound sense of inner peace.

Fortunately, we don't leave this sense of peace and stillness and openness to God at the altar. We carry it with us. Once we've achieved an awareness of God, writes Isaac of Nineveh, the heart fills with "joy and wonder, [and] bursts forth abundantly with impulses of thanksgiving and gratitude . . . as a result of the inner impulse which is greatly stirred by wonder." The person brimming with an awareness of God will "raise his voice and utter praise insatiably," and "[f]rom then on . . . will be with God constantly, without any break, in continual prayer."

This, for the Sufis, is true *zikr*. What begins as a ritual or meditative device, often practiced with the voice and body, becomes a permanent state of experiencing the Presence of God. The soul remembers the divine touch that brought life to the body, the holy breath exhaled into the soul, the Word that uttered humankind into being.

Such a memory opens the soul to God, and with that glance into eternity, we're forever on the path of love and longing that leads us to God.

CHAPTER TEN

Choosing My Mystic Path

*S*hortly after my book, *A Baptist Among the Jews*, was published, a popular, local radio host invited me, along with one of my Jewish friends, Dr. Karen Prager, to be guests on his program. After our thirty-minute discussion, listeners began calling in. Most people wanted to know if my theology changed when I became involved with Judaism, if I planned to convert, and how I handled discussions of Jesus.

One caller, however, directed his question towards Karen, who's a psychology professor at a local university. "I'm wondering," he said, "if you think Mary is suffering from cognitive dissonance."

It was a logical question. Many people whose beliefs have changed, or who are involved with more than one religion, experience what cognitive dissonance implies: unease or tension when their current beliefs are contradicted by new information. Some of my beliefs had indeed changed, and many of them through my relationship with Judaism, but I had never experienced dis-ease as a result of the change.

Instead, I felt a sense of joy and happiness. My ideas about and experience of God expanded. I'm far less legalistic, find meaning in Jewish ritual, and I love studying and worshiping with my Jewish friends.

Now, as I look back on my life from the perspective of several years further down the road, I suspect the caller would be even more baffled by my spiritual life. I'm still an active member of my church, attending services, chairing a committee. I attend Jewish prayer services as often as I attend church. But now I also practice *zikr* with a small group of Sufis on Wednesday nights.

Perhaps I haven't experienced the cognitive dissonance the caller expected because I've come to a place in my life where I simply want to experience and love and encounter God. The *cognitive* aspect of my spirituality is less important than it used to be. When I'm in church, I encounter God's presence. When I go to synagogue, I inhale God's presence. When I'm with the Sufis, I receive God's presence. For me, that's what religion—or spirituality—is all about.

Earlier in my life, I argued theology, often in a contentious manner, believing it was my mission to teach what I "knew" to be true. Now I cherish questions, primarily because of the influence Judaism has had on me. I believe that other people and other religions hold truth, too, and I long to learn from them and to experience God in new ways as a result of my relationship with others. I'm tired of arguing theology. Now I simply want to know God, in the intimate, biblical sense.

For various reasons, church will probably always feel like my family. There, I can talk freely about my spiritual interests and experiences. I've attended churches since I was two weeks old and in the best of these, I find people who accept me for who I am. I feel free to express myself. I feel at home. In other churches where my experiences weren't as happy, I've still found many good and loving people, happy times, joyful memories, and profound lessons.

Because of my long-time religious isolation, however, my awe and joy over discovering new truths has been intense. Recently, while attending a prayer service at Temple Emanu-El in Dallas, I couldn't stop crying. Two weeks later, I wept throughout another service. When someone recently asked me why Judaism moved me so deeply, I replied that I could give him a list of the things I loved, or I could put it this simply: I fell in love with your religion.

Sufism, however, has provided the active mystical path I crave. While all mystical paths have rituals and prayers whose purpose is to lead you into a direct encounter with God, Sufis meet regularly to participate together in these rituals. The state of ecstatic union mystics seek is brief (though it can occur repeatedly), but it leaves you forever changed. Like Isaiah, you're taken entirely outside of yourself and can only say with the angels, "Holy! Holy! Holy!" The world beyond merges with the world in which we live and all we've ever *thought* about God is subsumed in experiencing the *presence* of God.

I've had only a mere taste of what the greatest mystics were continually filled with, but Sufism has been the path where I've most vividly had this taste. Here, in this chapter, I'll tell you what drew me there and how it has changed my life.

....

Undoubtedly, for me, the most powerful draw of Sufism is its emphasis on love as the path to God. Like most people in the West, the little I knew about Sufism some years ago was through reading Rumi, but his poetry so attracted me that I had to know more. For Rumi, God was the Beloved, and a passionate longing and love for God filled every fiber and cell of his being. Once you sip the wine of God, say the Sufis, you'll drink until nothing else matters.

This is the ecstasy that Rumi continuously lived in. In his consuming love for God, Rumi wrote of: Rid[ing] the Moon and becoming the "endless Sea."

In the lover's heart is a lute
Which plays the melody of longing.
You say he looks crazy—
That's only because your ears are not tuned
To the music by which he dances.

He also wrote:

For me, the anguish inspired by your charms is
Inexhaustibly charming.
As the sun you blind me with the radiance of your beauty;
If I lower my gaze, who shall I look at?

Rumi epitomizes what it means to love God with all your heart, soul, and mind. Although this is a process, mystics often have a series of visions, encounters, or awakenings (epiphanies that cause you to suddenly see in a remarkable new way) that propel them down the path toward an utter absorption with God. In between these steps up the ladder (to use the metaphor of several Christian mystics) lies the work of daily remembrance: *zikr,* the spiritual discipline that gradually opens your heart to receive God's glory.

Rumi's encounter with Shams is often credited with changing him from a mere scholar to a passionate lover of God, but in truth, Rumi was already a holy man and a lover of God, and to some degree, had already been on the Sufi path. His meeting with Shams was simply the ultimate and final encounter that filled him to the brim with the Divine Embrace and forever altered the course of his life. Continuous mindfulness of God doesn't come overnight, and it didn't come that way for Rumi. His heart was, day by day, being made pure and ready and open so that when the Divine appeared, Rumi was capable of perceiving.

Recently, I read a column in which a Christian suggested that the church hadn't done well in defining love and because of this, love had become for many, little more than a "group hug." I agree that we haven't defined it, but that's because love is undefinable. Who can understand love but one who has experienced it? In my opinion, the problem is not that we've made love too mushy; it's that we sometimes don't make it mushy enough!

Yes, love *is* a feeling—a very deep, passionate feeling. It's strong enough to see beauty in another that no one else sees; it overlooks faults, and it patiently rides out difficult situations. A passionate lover doesn't do this out of a sense of duty or through discipline; he does it because his heart allows nothing else.

For the Sufis, love is not only the divine force that draws the worshiper toward God, it is the full realization, goal, and culmination of the spiritual path. In other words, love begets more love until, as the apostle John says, "love is perfected in us." "Sufism," writes Llewellyn Vaughan-Lee, "is suited to those who need to realize their relationship with God as a love affair, who need to be drawn by the thread of love and longing back to their Beloved." This particularly appeals to me because of the legalism that had marked most of my life.

This morning I sat at the altar in my home and realized how full of worship I felt. *Al-Azim,* I said, fingering my first prayer bead, *al-Jalil.* The Magnificent, The Majestic. The Magnificent, The Majestic. Filled with love, I was reminded, once again, why I'm drawn to the mystical path of Sufism.

. . . .

Another reason Sufism attracts me is, of course, its absorption in mystery. I'm deeply drawn to the mysterious, to aspects of God that rise above my intellectual grasp, and to realms of experience that bring God into my life in an out-of-the-ordinary way.

One afternoon, not long ago, one of my dear friends Melanie Brown and I were having lunch after church when she began to talk about her only sister's death some years back. Her sister, Patti, had loved butterflies, Melanie said, and when she was alive, had filled her backyard with various flowers that attracted them. Patti never tired of watching these butterflies as they fluttered through her yard and gardens.

At a young age, Patti got cancer, and the loss Melanie felt devastated her. Before Patti's death, though, an amazing and strange thing happened. As the family sat together one afternoon in a park, a flock of butterflies landed on Patti. "They didn't touch anyone except for Patti," Melanie told me, "and they illuminated her body." Later, for Melanie, the appearance of a butterfly brought a divine message of comfort—a lovely and tangible sign that linked this world to the one beyond.

I listened to Melanie's story in awe over the mysteries and divine whispers of comfort and guidance that sometimes invade our daily lives and surprise us with glimpses of a world beyond our senses and intellectual understanding. "What a beautiful, breathtaking experience," I whispered to Melanie.

"It was an amazing moment," Melanie agreed. "I'm glad I could tell you about it. A lot of people think that seeing divine messages in things like that makes you strange or even a little crazy."

Most of us want to appear "normal," yet in the Sufi tradition, the general populace often branded dervishes, who experienced the wonders of the spiritual world, as insane.

Likewise, in Judaism. In one story about the Ba'al Shem Tov, the founder of Hasidism, a supposedly "crazy" woman recognized and accepted his miraculous powers at a time when most people reviled and rejected him.

During my lunch this afternoon I was reading the newspaper when an article popped out at me about the increasing numbers of people who are taking on "trained guides" to help them on their spiritual paths. The article stated that training centers now exist in forty-one states, and it explained how the roles of spiritual guides differ from that of pastors and rabbis. What caught my eye, however, was a disclaimer made by one of the women interviewed for the article.

When asked to describe *spiritual direction*, she hastened to assure readers what it *isn't*. "It isn't about having visions or unusual phenomenon," she said. Commenting on this, the writer added that the woman hoped to "assuage those wondering if the practice is 'woo woo.'"

I guess I can't get away from it, I mused to myself, as I read the article. *I'm attracted to "woo woo."* And yes, there are dangers associated with "woo woo." Some people, for instance, continually look for miraculous signs and are either paralyzed with indecision when they don't come, or flounder off in too many and often unwise directions when they latch onto every sign as some kind of "clear voice" of divine guidance.

Yet while those of us who are mystically inclined do indeed value our spiritual intuition and take note of our dreams, visions, and other supernatural signs that enter our lives, we also take many other factors into consideration when making a decision: "[T]est the spirits to see whether they are from God," warns the apostle John, and St. Paul echoes this: "[T]est everything; hold fast to what is good; abstain from every form of evil."

Thus, the mystic takes serious note of a supernatural sign only if it's in line with what the Sufis call *haqq*, or Truth. Is the "sign" pointing towards something selfish or egoistic? If so, something's wrong. Usually, a number of indications and signs, including a deep conviction, will let us know that the decision we're about to make is the right one. In my life, mystical experiences sometimes merely confirm a decision I'm already strongly leaning toward making.

I've also received epiphanies that have moved me into a more intense awareness of the presence of God, or inexplicable events that have eased intense and lingering doubts, hurts, and anger or bitterness.

One of my own most memorable experiences came a few years ago when I had decided to stop writing. I had enjoyed a good deal of success writing for periodicals but had unsuccessfully struggled for several years as I tried to break into books. In my frustration, I began to think about a new career and to assess my other talents and work experience. For a couple of weeks, I spent mornings browsing through the classified ads for job opportunities.

Then one morning I woke up earlier than usual with a powerful sense of God's presence in the room. As I lay there, a voice that seemed almost audible spoke to my heart. No matter how long it takes, I heard, my life's purpose right now was to write books. I got up and headed for my computer, but before I reached it, the phone rang. It was a publisher, interested in a book I had earlier proposed. Before I had *even set the phone down,* another publisher called, asking me if I'd be interested in writing a travel book. Over the course of the next two weeks, four additional publishers called to talk about four different books!

Then, a week after my epiphany, another strange event happened. I had spent an evening with several people in meditation and had had a vision of a llama, which symbolizes certain spiritual qualities such as confident climbing at steep "altitudes," handing me a gift inside a jeweled box. Hours later, getting into my car, a message alert sounded on my mobile phone—a call from yet another publisher. Something told me, however, that this was the one.

I had been excited about the others, but I'd also had doubts about all of them. When I listened to this message, however, there were no doubts. I wanted to write this book. I checked the time of the message and though I didn't know the precise time of my vision, I did know that the message had been left within a few minutes of it. The book, *A Baptist Among the Jews*, was written, published, and featured on television and radio programs all over the country.

There have been other epiphanies, other voices from beyond, that have had an equally powerful effect on my life. One of these occurred only a few days ago as I sat at the altar in my home meditating. I had finished *zikr* and was sitting quietly, thinking I should pray for Mike, who had been feeling an unusually deep sense of depression and discouragement over the past few months.

As I began to pray, I had a distinct feeling that I should, instead, continue to sit quietly and open my heart to God. Again, an almost audible voice made it clear that my past way of praying was actually a cop-out, an avoidance of responsibility. Rather than saying, "Dear God, please help Mike with his depression," God wanted me to be filled with a fresh wave of love and compassion and to offer this to Mike not through a verbal prayer, but through my own heartfelt actions.

Mike's moods had been wearing on me, and so listening to the voice that told me to stop praying for him and to instead open my own heart to the fullness of God, and to offer that to Mike, was much more difficult than the simple prayer I'd planned to voice. But it was the path of a new level of consciousness and understanding in the meaning of prayer.

My decision to have my own heart filled and to turn my prayer into action increased my maturity, deepened my love and compassion, gave Mike a fuller sense of God's presence, and strengthened our relationship. I doubt that I'll ever approach prayer in the same way again. God had moved me, through a life-changing epiphany, into a deeper understanding of what prayer is—an opening of the heart that allows *me* to be transformed and to embody God's love and kindness and mercy to others.

"Signs and wonders" aren't anything to brag about. In fact, Baba encourages us to speak of them only when doing so will clearly help or guide someone else. Otherwise, we tend to measure our spirituality or to feel prideful over the miraculous interventions that come into our lives.

I like St. Teresa's response to the many mystical occurrences in her own life. She constantly had to answer the harsh criticism and mistrust of the other nuns, as well as that of some of her spiritual directors, and though she was repeatedly accused before the Inquisition, Teresa remained firm but humble. Without denying her visions and ecstatic trances, Teresa told her confessor that she thought these were given to her as "a means . . . for my salvation since I saw I was so wretched. For good people don't have need of so much in order to serve His Majesty."

In reality, of course, saints (along with the not-so-saintly) do indeed receive supernatural interventions from God, as Teresa's own life showed. When we open ourselves to mysteries and divine occurrences, we usually receive them. The important thing is that we seek God, not the mystical experiences, and that we don't feel a sense of pride when we receive them.

·········

It's a sunny, beautiful afternoon in March and about twenty of us are gathered at Risa Ranch in Austin, Texas, sitting on couches, windowsills, pillows, rolled-up blankets, and stairwells in the living room, engaged in *sohbet* with Baba. I whisper to the woman next to me that it's hard not to just sit and stare at Baba's radiant face and she whispers back that she doesn't try not to. Baba's face reflects his extraordinary heart.

The weekend is drawing to a close and it's time for lunch. We're all tired, including Baba, but a woman named Candace asks if we'd like to end our time with music. Jem translates the question to Baba and Baba enthusiastically nods his head. Candace pulls her guitar from the case and we begin to sing.

A salaam alaykhum, alaykhum a salaam; a salaam alaykhum, alaykhum a salaam. (*Peace be with you and with you be peace.*) Although Baba had a stroke some years ago, has had a long weekend giving to us, and was tired and hungry, he jumped in after three songs. "Continue!" he says in English. "I like!" Candace led us in a fourth song and Baba asked, again in English, "Finish? Done? No! Continue! I'm hungry for music, not for food." Baba then asks for the song to be sung in Hebrew.

Baba often explains a famous saying of Rumi's, which I've already mentioned, but which, with your permission (as Baba says), I'll tell again. . . .

"Mevlana [Rumi] was raised as a Muslim but when he said, 'Come come!' he wasn't calling people to Islam. He was calling out to all peoples to embrace each other in love and unity, and to spread the light of God."

This is the love of Sufism, it is the love of Sherif Baba, and it is the love that I long to live and breathe and share with the world.

GLOSSARY

ascent: path of the mystic's return to God as he or she travels through various levels of consciousness or mystical "worlds." St. John of the Cross compares this to climbing "a ladder of love."

ashk: divine love

Baba: a Turkish term of affection meaning "Dad"

dergah: a place where dervishes gather and where the tombs of other dervishes lie

dervish: one who has been initiated as a Sufi

Divine Name: ninety-nine in Sufism; one or more are chanted during *zikr*, the Sufi ritual of Divine Remembrance

dhikr: see *zikr*

emanation: the idea that various levels of creation flowed from God

fana: loss of our egos as we join in union with God

initiate: one who has been accepted by a teacher into the path of Sufism; usually this acceptance is recognized through a ceremony

mevlana: "master"—name by which Turkish Sufis refer to Rumi

muhasaba: self-analysis

mureed: Sufi initiate

murshid: Sufi master

order: various branches of Sufism

Rumi: Persia's most well-known poet; known as Mevlana in Turkey

sema: the ecstatic whirling movement created through the divine friendship of Rumi and Shams

shaykh: spiritual teacher (female teachers are known as *shaykha*)

sohbet: spiritual discourse—a time when Sufi masters spontaneously offer teaching, invite feedback and answer questions

Sufism: the mystical practice that emphasizes certain unique rituals for guiding spiritual seekers into a direct encounter with God

union: the merging of one's deepest self with God

zikr: Divine Remembrance of God, consisting of the repetition of the ninety-nine Divine Names of God

ACKNOWLEDGMENTS

Thanks to Jem Williford and Wahhaba Phillips for answering countless questions.

Thanks to Claudia Barner, Margaret Hejny, Shirin Kaye-Sacek, Lamia Laura Via, Tim Mahoney, Belkis, Hadiya Vail, and Wahhaba Phillips for reading this manuscript in such a short time frame and for offering invaluable suggestions.

To my Wednesday night group—Wahhaba, Kabir, Yahiya, Sarah, and Joan—your love and commitment bring beauty into the world.

Tim Mahoney, you recreated both the mind and heart of ancient philosophy in the modern classroom. A dry moment never dared enter there. Little wonder that you instilled in me a fascination with mysticism.

To honor the memory of the last Caravan of the Beautiful, Austin, Texas, May 2004 . . . I'll miss you. Deborah, Margaret, Don, Leilah, and so many others, you helped make the Caravan beautiful.

The community in Chapel Hill, North Carolina . . . Shirin, Belkis, Shekibe, Lamia, Jem, Ceyda, Hadiya, Bedria, and others— thanks for making me feel so welcome. You are beautiful friends. Soltan, your exuberant joy is contagious. Demir, your help and hospitality at Rumi Fest saved the day. Blessings to all of you for sharing Baba!

Jem, thanks for making it possible for me to experience Sufism all over Turkey. Shekibe, Shirin, and Lamia, thanks for being great roommates and friends, also. John Brozak, a special hug for you for your friendship and help in Turkey.

Thank you to the many dervishes in Turkey who are among the most hospitable people I've ever met. To everyone at Ummi Sinan and Dogancay, thank you for welcoming and caring for me.

Lil Copan, you're a joy to work with. To everyone at Paraclete Press, thank you for bringing this book to fruition.

Mike, thanks for moving through life with me with such love and support. I couldn't make it without you.

Mom, thank you for instilling in me such a powerful sense of God's love. Dad, I know you're dancing through the universe.

Wilshire, especially George, Phil, Claudia, Ann, and the Compass Class—you saved my life when I was drowning.

Shahabuddin David Less, you've been a guide, a light, and a mirror in my life.

Sherif Baba, who initiated me into the mystical path of Sufism, your purity, buoyant delight with life, lack of judgment, and love for everyone, despite their race, religion, or choices in life, inspires me and moves me into the deepest realms of the Divine. To know you is to love you.

NOTES

CHAPTER ONE

p. 5   *[The Sufi Movement has] members . . . which belong . . .* Khan, *The Sufi Message*, 271.

p. 5   *"Teacher, which commandment in the law . . . "* Matthew 22:36–40.

p. 5   *Rumi, who is currently America's best-selling poet, . . .* Zabor, *The Turn*, 61.

p. 6   *O lovers! O lovers!* Quoted from Ibn Arabi in, *Rumi: In the Arms of the Beloved*, xviii.

CHAPTER TWO

p. 10   *This state of consciousness shatters and transforms us. . . .* paraphrased from Cooper, *Three Gates to Meditation Practice*, x.

p. 10   *. . . ecstasy as a state of purity in which our hearts . . .* paraphrased from Khan, *The Music of Life*, 30.

p. 10   *his heart received the meaning and power . . .* St. Bonaventure, *The Life of St. Francis*, 18.

p. 11   *Oh, I absorb the shining!* and *Dance when you are broken open. . . .* Olmsted, *Songs of Rumi*, tracks 10-11.

p. 14   *music [drags] God from His slumbers . . .* Bobin, *The Secret of St. Francis*, 17.

CHAPTER THREE

p. 23   *"deeply from the heart . . ."* Deuteronomy 10:16; Psalm 111:1; 1 Peter 1:22.

p. 23   *Drain passion's cup, . . .* Rumi, *Rumi's Divan of Shems of Tabriz*, 135.

p. 24   *One day Rumi sat teaching a group of students. . . .* paraphrased from Bayat and Jamnia, *Tales from the Land of the Sufis*, 127-28 (reprinted by arrangement with Shambhala Publications, Inc., Boston, www.shambhala.com).

p. 25   *It is said that the Great Maggid . . .* Gafni, *The Mystery of Love*, 36.

p. 25   *knowledge of the law . . .* paraphrased from Romans 7:9–11.

p. 25   *"The heart is the faculty by which one knows God. . . ."* Baker and Henry, *Merton and Sufism*, excerpt in front of book.

p. 25   *The heart is the seat of consciousness of God.* . . . Bakhtiar, *Moral Healing*, xiv (emphasis mine).

p. 26   *Then one day Moses came by and heard* . . . paraphrased from Bayat and Jamnia, *Tales for the Land of the Sufis*, 142–44 (reprinted by arrangement with Shambhala Publications, Inc., Boston, www.shambhala.com).

p. 26   *The heart that the apostle Paul in the Greek Testament* . . . I refer to the two testaments of Scripture as the Hebrew Testament and Greek Testament, reflecting the languages in which they were originally written.

p. 26   *sighs too deep for words* . . . Romans 8:26.

p. 26   *"The pure in heart will see God. . . ."* Matthew 5:8.

p. 27   *Mrs. Jameson.* This name has been changed to protect privacy.

p. 30   *At the center of our being* . . . Baker and Henry, *Merton and Sufism*, 67.

p. 32   *The goal of zikr is beautifully illustrated in the story* . . . Bayat and Jamnia, *Tales for the Land of the Sufis*, 46 (reprinted by arrangement with Shambhala Publications, Inc., Boston, www.shambhala.com).

p. 32   *"If I were to be responsible for guiding souls . . ."* Brother Lawrence, *Practice of the Presence*, 30.

CHAPTER FOUR

p. 34   *"Why do you see the speck . . . "* Matthew 7:3.

p. 34   *"rent by the violence of love."* Rumi, *Teachings of Rumi*, 2.

p. 34   *Hazrat Inayat Khan, the Indian master* . . . paraphrased from Khan, *The Music of Life*, 319.

p. 35   *The fire of love burns so intensely. . . .* Bayat and Jamnia, *Tales from the Land of the Sufis*, 117, 35 (reprinted by arrangement with Shambhala Publications, Inc., Boston, www.shambhala.com).

p. 36   *Through the writers of the New Testament* . . . paraphrased from Howe, *Passionate Love*, 54. (For a fuller study on the Greek words for love, see my article in *Mars Hill Review*.)

p. 36   *The apostle Paul speaks of a love fulfilled with joy and longing.* . . . paraphrased from Philippians 4:1.

p. 36   *The apostle Peter tells us to love deeply. . . .* paraphrased from 1 Peter 1:22.

p. 36   *Be drunk, on Love* . . . Rumi, *Rumi's Divan of Shems of Tabriz*, 75, 67.

p. 36   *Love is the endless ocean of God. . . .* Rumi, *Rumi: In the Arms of the Beloved*, 82.

p. 37   *The subject tonight is Love. . . .* Hafiz, *The Subject Tonight is Love*, 27, 47.

p. 37   *John Michael Talbot, the Franciscan musician and author . . .*
        Talbot, *The Fire of God,* viii-ix.

p. 37   *large golden dart . . .* St. Teresa, *The Collected Works,* 252.

p. 38   *"Kiss[ing] their hands and their faces . . ."* St. Bonaventure,
        The Life of St. Francis of Assisi, 15-16.

p. 39   *My spirit faints with longing.* Psalm 143:7 NIV.

p. 39   *intense longing for God . . .* Palmer, Sherrard, and Ware, trans.
        and eds., *The Philokalia,* 54.

p. 39   *In one story the Sufis tell of a devoted man . . .* Olmsted, *Songs
        of Rumi,* (CD), track #6, "Love Dogs."

p. 40   *Though I am in the fire of hell . . .* Rumi, *Fountain of Fire,* 27.

p. 40   *If your mind and stomach burn . . .* Rumi, *Rumi: In the Arms
        of the Beloved,* 154.

p. 40   *longing and desire are good . . .* Gafni, *The Mystery of Love,*
        33-4.

p. 41   *In one of Deepak Chopra's imaginative and humorous stories . . .*
        paraphrased from Chopra, *The Way of the Wizard,* 119.

p. 41   *What disguises He wears . . .* Rumi, *Rumi's Divan of Shems of
        Tabriz,* 91.

p. 42   *Do not despair if the Beloved pushes you away, . . .* Rumi,
        Rumi: In the Arms of the Beloved, 94.

p. 42   *"Teacher, which commandment in the law . . . ?"* Matthew 22:
        36–40.

p. 42   *God is love.* 1 John 4:16b.

p. 44   *Bayat and Jamnia show us the transforming power of longing . . .*
        Bayat and Jamnia, *Takes from the Land of the Sufis,* 71-80
        (reprinted by arrangement with Shambhala Publications,
        Inc., Boston, www.shambhala.com).

p. 44   *What no eye has seen, nor ear heard . . .* 1 Corinthians 2:9-10.

p. 44   *Spirit searches . . .* 1 Corinthians 2:10.

p. 44   *Paul, the man who had life-altering visions . . .*
        2 Corinthians 12:2; Romans 8:26.

CHAPTER FIVE

p. 47   *In his Degrees of the Soul Shaykh abd al-Khalig al-
        Shawbrawi . . .* al-Shabrawi, *The Degrees of the Soul,* 5, 15.

p. 48   *If you were to be in a state of sincerity . . .* al-Iskandari, *The
        Key of Salvation,* 68.

p. 49   *This level of purity is illustrated in the story . . .* Khan, *Tales,*
        55-6.

p. 49   *his human righteousness was as "filthy rags" . . .* Isaiah 64:6.

p. 49   *The fruit of the Spirit is . . .* Galatians 5:22-3.

p. 49   *things that are true, honorable, just . . .* Philippians 4:8.

p. 50   *This kind of inner purity involves* . . . al-Shabrawi, *The Degrees of the Soul*, 5.

p. 51   *In compassion and grace be like sun.* A friend has pointed out that since Turkish has no articles, English translations are often grammatically incorrect. I've left the wording as it appears on my prints, however, because to me it sounds lovely.

p. 51   *Either exist as you are or be as you look.* A better (or at least more common) translation for this, I'm told, is "Either appear as you are or be as you appear."

CHAPTER SIX

p. 61   *In* Spiritual Dance and Walk *Samuel Lewis gives a key* . . . Lewis, *Spiritual Dance and Walk*, 70–72.

p. 61   *The music should accentuate the natural rhythm.* . . . Lewis, *Spiritual Dance and Walk*, 71.

p. 62   *Certain movements promote the translucent Angelic moods.* . . . Lewis, *Spiritual Dance and Walk*, 30, 23.

p. 63   *There's a powerful sense of energy* . . . Gass and Brehony, *Chanting*, 89-90.

p. 63   *The dervishes* . . . *slowly walk around the room* . . . Bayat and Jamnia, *Tales from the Land of the Sufis*, 130 (reprinted by arrangement with Shambhala Publications, Inc., Boston, www.shambhala.com).

p. 63   *These forces are aroused when the body rotates.* . . .Khan, *Awakening*, 168.

p. 64   *How imprinted upon my heart and mind is an evening* . . . A *dergah* is a place where dervishes gather and where the tombs of other dervishes lie. At *Ummi Sinan*, though the bodies have been moved to a graveyard, the tombs remain; thus, it's still considered a *dergah*, as opposed to a *tekke*, which contains no tombs.

p. 65   *First they [the cobras] come out of the hole* . . . Khan, *The Music of Life*, 272-73.

CHAPTER SEVEN

p. 67   *away from the body* . . . 2 Corinthians 5:8.

p. 69   *When someone imagines himself to have any kind of perfection,* . . . al-Shabrawi, *The Degrees of the Soul*, 9, 29.

p. 69   *The person who is proud of his spiritual progress,* . . . Palmer, Sherrard, and Ware, *Philokalia*, 57.

p. 69   *St. Teresa of Avila wrote that perhaps God* . . . St. Teresa, *The Collected Works*, 432.

p. 69   *[p]ride in making spiritual progress must be checked . . .*
            Pseudo-Macarius, *Pseudo-Macarius*, 16.

p. 70   *When modern-day author Paul Mariani spent thirty days . . .*
            Mariani, *Thirty Days*, 8-9.

p. 70   *practices tailored to [a person's] level of spiritual understanding*
            . . . Ray, *Secret of the Vajra World*, 17.

p. 73   *St. John of the Cross compares the ascent to climbing "a ladder*
            of love," . . . St. John of the Cross, *Dark Night of the Soul*,
            167, 174-75.

p. 73   *For the Jewish mystic, the Most Holy Name is YHWH . . .*
            Jacobs, *Jewish Mystical Testimonies*, 62.

p. 73   *Sikhs also commune and draw closer to God through repetition*
            of God's names. . . . Singh, *The Name of My Beloved*, 7.

p. 73   *Hindus—a practice they refer to as* namajapa *. . .* Bruteau,
            The Other Half of My Soul, 56.

p. 73   *God "is not power, nor is [God] light. . . nor is [God] eternity*
            or time, . . ." Pseudo-Dionysius, *The Complete Works*, 140-41.

p. 74   *. . . we use metaphors to describe God only when our souls need*
            something "to hold onto. . ." Brock, *The Syriac Fathers on*
            Prayer, 257-58.

p. 74   *. . . the aspect of Sufism that most deeply attracted Thomas*
            Merton . . . Baker, *Merton and Sufism*, 44-45.

p. 74   *Joseph the Visionary, among others, wrote of* msarquta. . . .
            Brock, *The Syriac Fathers on Prayer*, xxxi.

p. 75   *Chittister tells of a recent interview . . .* Chittester, *Spirituality*
            and Health, 31-32.

p. 75   *we return to the earth "radically transformed . . .* Özturk, *The*
            Eye of the Heart, 26.

p. 76   *Hazrat Inayat Khan tells the story of the Sufi master . . .* Khan,
            Tales, 32-33.

CHAPTER EIGHT

p. 78   *To be guided by a mature and advanced spiritual soul-friend . . .*
            Pseudo-Macarius, *Pseudo-Macarius*, 17.

p. 78   *Eastern Buddhists remind us that when we meditate . . .* Ray,
            Secret of the Vajra World, 76.

p. 81   *. . . the most important teaching that the Sufi master passes*
            on . . . Vaughan-Lee, *Sufism, the Transformation of the Heart*, 6.

p. 81   *[E]nlightened knowledge can be transmitted from one person to*
            another, . . . www.pcddallas.org.

CHAPTER NINE

p. 89   *"Lord, make me an instrument of . . ."* Talbot, Master
         Collection Disc 2,   Track 8.

p. 90   *Hazrat Inayat Khan reminds us that human beings affect the*
         atmospheric . . . Khan, *The Music of Life,* 15, 23.

p. 91   *And all of us, with unveiled faces . . .* 2 Corinthians 3:18.

p. 93   *One suggestion for this* zikr, *or meditation, . . .* Barks and
         Green, *The Illuminated Prayer,* 122.97. Baker and Henry,
         Merton and Sufism, 37.

p. 93   *hesychastic:* One who practices the still, interior prayer of
         the heart.

p. 93   *Merton explained to his novices . . .* Baker and Henry, *Merton*
         and Sufism, 37.

p. 94   *In the late 1700s, a German physicist, Ernst Chladni, . . .*
         Cunningham, *Mandala: Journey to the Center,* 31.

p. 94   *[I]s God the God of Jews only?* Romans 3:29-30.

p. 97   *I think of the prophet Isaiah's vision of God, . . .* see Isaiah
         6:1–7.

p. 97   *We are that temple.* 1 Corinthians 3:16.

p. 98   *Once we've achieved an awareness of God, writes Isaac of*
         Nineveh, . . . Brock, *The Syriac Fathers on Prayer,* 249-50.

CHAPTER TEN

p. 102   *Rid[ing] the Moon and becoming the "endless Sea." . . .*
         Rumi, *Rumi: In the Arms of the Beloved,* 69.

p. 102   *For me, the anguish inspired by your charms . . .* Rumi,
         Rumi's Divan of Shems of Tabriz, 117.

p. 102   *In between these steps up the ladder . . .* St. John of
         the Cross, John Climacus (John of the Ladder), St. Bernard,
         and St. Thomas Aquinas, for instance.

p. 103   *love is perfected in us . . . .* 1 John 4:12

p. 103   *Sufism, writes Llewellyn Vaughan-Lee, is suited . . .*
         Vaughan- Lee, *Sufism, the Transformatioon of the Heart,* 4.

p. 105   *[T]est the spirits. . . . .* 1 John 4:1

p. 105   *[T]est everything. . . . .* 1 Thessalonians 5:21-22

p. 108   *I like St. Teresa's response to the many mystical occurrences*
         . . . St. Teresa, *The Collected Works,* 27, 432.

BIBLIOGRAPHY

al-Iskandari, Ibn Ata Allah. *The Key to Salvation*. Cambridge, U.K.: The Islamic Texts Society, 1996.

al-Shabrawi, Shaykh abd al-Khaliq. *The Degrees of the Soul*. London: The Quilliam Press Limited, 1997.

Baker, Rob, and Gray Henry, eds. *Merton and Sufism*. Louisville, KY: Fons Vitae, 1999.

Bakhtiar, Laleh. *Moral Healing Through the Most Beautiful Names*, vol. 3. Chicago: The Institute of Traditional Psychoethics and Guidance, 1994.

Barks, Coleman, and Michael Green. *The Illuminated Prayer*. New York: The Ballantine Publishing Group, 2000.

Bayat, Mojdeh, and Mohammad Ali Jamnia. *Tales from the Land of the Sufis*. Boston, MA: Shambhala Publications, 1994.

Bobin, Christian. *The Secret of Francis of Assisi*. Boston, MA: Shambhala Publications, 1997.

Brock, Sebastian, intro & trans. *The Syriac Fathers on Prayer and the Spiritual Life*. Kalamazoo, MI: Cistercian Publications, Inc., 1987.

Brother Lawrence. *The Practice of the Presence of God*. Springdale, PA: Whitaker House, 1982.

Bruteau, Beatrice, comp. *The Other Half of my Soul (Bede Griffiths and the Hindu-Christian Dialogue)*. Wheaton, IL: Quest Books, 1996.

Chittister, Joan D. "How Shall We Live?" *Spirituality & Health* (Nov./Dec. 2003): 31-32.

Chopra, Deepak. *The Way of the Wizard*. New York: Harmony Books, 1995.

Cooper, David A. *Three Gates to Meditation Practice*. Woodstock, VT: Skylight Paths Publishing, 2000.

Cunningham, Bailey. *Mandala: Journey to the Center*. New York: DK Publishing, 2002.

Gafni, Marc. *The Mystery of Love*. New York: Atrai Books, 2003.

Gass, Robert, and Kathleen Brehony. *Chanting*. New York: Broadway Books, 1999.

Hafiz. (vers. by D. Ladinsky). *The Subject Tonight is Love*. North Myrtle Beach, SC: Pumpkin House Press, 1996.

Howe, Mary Blye. "Passionate Love." *Mars Hill Review* (Summer 1998): 54-55.

Jacobs, Louis. *Jewish Mystical Testimonies*. New York: Schocken Books, 1977.

Khan, Hazrat Inayat. *Mastery*. New Lebanon, NY: Omega Publications, 1985.

———. *The Music of Life*. New Lebanon, NY: Omega Publications, 1983.

———. *Tales*. New Lebanon, NY: Omega Publications, 1991.

———. *The Sufi Message of Hazrat Inayat Khan,* vol. 60, *The Unity of Religious Ideals*. London: Barrie and Rockliff, 1963.

Khan, Pir Vilayat Inayat Khan. *Awakening*. New York: Jeremy P. Tarcher/Putnam, 1999.

Lewis, Samuel L. *Spiritual Dance and Walk*. Seattle, WA: PeaceWorks, 1990.

Mariani, Paul. *Thirty Days*. New York: Viking, 2002.

Murchison, William. "Gibson's Christ doesn't go over well with liberals." *Dallas Morning News* (March 6, 2004): 29a.

Olmsted, Jeff. *Songs of Rumi: Don't Go Back to Sleep* (CD). Trans. by Coleman Barks, 2001: InspoPop.com.

Özturk, Yaşar Nuri. *The Eye of the Heart*. Istanbul: Redhouse Press, 1988.

Palmer, G.E.H., Philip Sherrard, and Kallistos Ware, trans. & eds. *The Philokalia*. London: Faber and Faber, 1981.

Palyul Changchub Dargyeling Dallas. *Meaning of Sangha (Practice Group)*. www.pcddallas.org.

Pseudo-Dionysius (trans. C. Luibheid). *Pseudo-Dionysius: The Complete Works*. New York: Paulist Press, 1987.

Pseudo-Macarius (trans., ed. & intro. S. J. Maloney) *Pseudo-Macarius*. New York: Paulist Press, 1992.

Ray, Reginald A. *Secret of the Vajra World*. Boston: Shambhala Publications, 2001.

Rumi. *Fountain of Fire*. Hesperia, CA: Cal-Earth Press, 1994 (copyright 1994, Nader Khalili).

———. (trans. J. Star). *Rumi: In the Arms of the Beloved*. New York: Penguin Putnam, 1997.

———. *Rumi's Divan of Shems of Tabriz*. Rockport, MA: Element Books, 1997.

———. (trans. E. Whinfield) *Teachings of Rumi: The Masnavi*. London, The Octagon Press, 1979.

Seal, Jeremy. *A Fez of the Heart*. San Diego, New York, London: Harcourt Brace & Company, 1995.

Singh, Nikky-Guninder Kaur. *The Name of My Beloved*. New York: HarperCollins Publishers, 1995.

St. Bonaventure. *The Life of St. Francis of Assisi*. Rockford, IL: Tan Books and Publishers, 1988.

St. John of the Cross (trans. ed, and intro, by E. A. Peers). *Dark Night of the Soul*. New York: Doubleday, 1990.

St. Teresa of Avila (trans. K. Kavanaugh and O. Rodriguez). *The Collected Works,* vol. 1 Washington, D.C.: ICS Publications, 1987.

Talbot, John Michael. *The Fire of God*. New York: Crossroad Publishing Co., 1988.

——. *Master Collection,* vol. 1. Brentwood, TN: The Sparrow Corporation, 1989.

Vaughan-Lee, Llewellyn. *Sufism: The Transformation of the Heart.* Inverness, CA: The Golden Sufi Center, 1995.

Zabor, Rafi. "The Turn: Inside the Secret Dervish Orders of Istanbul." *Harper's Magazine* (June 2004).

ABOUT PARACLETE PRESS

WHO WE ARE

Paraclete Press is an ecumenical publisher of books on Christian spirituality for people of all denominations and backgrounds.

We publish books that represent the wide spectrum of Christian belief and practice—from Catholic to Evangelical to liturgical to Orthodox.

We market our books primarily through booksellers; we are what is called a "trade" publisher, which means that we like it best when readers buy our books from booksellers, our partners in successfully reaching as wide of an audience as possible.

We are uniquely positioned in the marketplace without connection to a large corporation or conglomerate and with informal relationships to many branches and denominations of faith, rather than a formal relationship to any single one. We focus on publishing a diversity of thoughts and perspectives—the fruit of our diversity as a company.

WHAT WE ARE DOING

Paraclete Press is publishing books that show the diversity and depth of what it means to be Christian. We publish books that reflect the Christian experience across many cultures, time periods, and houses of worship.

We publish books about spiritual practice, history, ideas, customs and rituals, and books that nourish the vibrant life of the church.

We have several different series of books within Paraclete Press, including the bestselling Living Library series of modernized classic texts, A Voice from the Monastery—giving voice to men and women monastics on what it means to live a spiritual life today, and Many Mansions—for exploring the riches of the world's religious traditions and discovering how other faiths inform Christian thought and practice.

Learn more about us at our website: www.paracletepress.com, or call us toll-free at (800) 451-5006.

ALSO PUBLISHED IN THE "MANY MANSIONS" SERIES . . .

LET US BREAK BREAD TOGETHER:
A Passover Haggadah for Christians
By Pastor Michael A. Smith
and Rabbi Rami Shapiro

ISBN: 1-55725-444-3
Paperback
64 pages
$8.95

Jews have been celebrating the Passover through a special meal, called a seder, for millenia. Jesus himself celebrated the Passover feast with his disciples in what we refer to as The Last Supper.

In this special book, co-authored by a rabbi and a pastor, you will have the unique opportunity to experience an authentic Jewish Passover seder, from a distinctively Christian perspective. You will experience this Jewish custom as a means of deepening your Christian faith, and better understanding the Jewishness of Jesus.

Always respectful of the differences between Judaism and Christianity, this Passover guide provides a plan and script for a Christian seder, and highlights the great themes of the Exodus story in combination with Christian insights. You will discover why Jesus placed such importance on the universal themes of slavery, freedom, and community around the seder table.

"At last, a truly usable guide for Christians who wish to include appropriate elements of Jewish tradition in their own worship experience! In *Let Us Break Break Together: A Passover Haggadah for Christians*, Mike Smith and Rami Shapiro have provided a readable and functional guide for the rapidly growing number of Christian families and churches who are including the observance of a Passover seder in their own traditions. Working in an atmosphere of openness and respect, this rabbi and pastor have provided an introduction to and pilot plan for creating a Christian celebration of Passover informed by a solid awareness of Jewish tradition."
—Dr. Robert O. Byrd
H. F. Paschall Chair of Biblical Studies and Preaching,
The School of Religion, Belmont University

Available from most booksellers or through Paraclete Press:
www.paracletepress.com; 1-800 451-5006.
Try your local bookstore first.